Jan 28

Garrett Biblical Institute
Evanston, Illinois

W9-DIT-677

378

378

The Cambridge Manuals of Science and
Literature

LIFE IN THE MEDIEVAL
UNIVERSITY

CAMBRIDGE UNIVERSITY PRESS

London: FETTER LANE, E.C.

C. F. CLAY, Manager

Edinburgh: 100 PRINCES STREET
Berlin: A. ASHER AND CO.
Leipzig: F. A. BROCKHAUS
New York: G. P. PUTNAM'S SONS
Bombay and Calcutta: MACMILLAN AND CO., Ltd.

All rights reserved

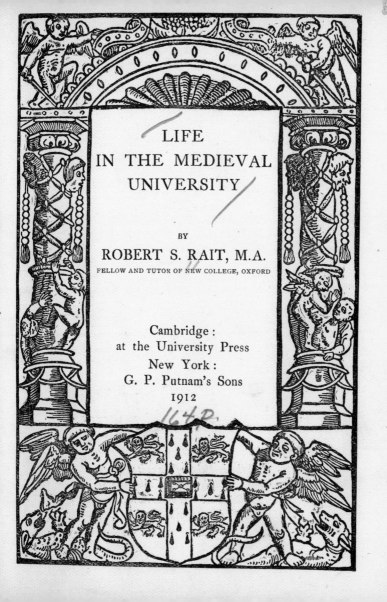

LIFE IN THE MEDIEVAL UNIVERSITY

BY

ROBERT S. RAIT, M.A.

FELLOW AND TUTOR OF NEW COLLEGE, OXFORD

Cambridge:
at the University Press
New York:
G. P. Putnam's Sons
1912

378

164 P.

Garrett Biblical Institute
Evanston, Illinois

With the exception of the coat of arms at the foot, the design on the title page is a reproduction of one used by the earliest known Cambridge printer, John Siberch, 1521

MAY 19 1921

LA177
·K16R
1912

Purchased

79839)

NOTE ON THE FRONTISPIECE

In this picture the schoolboy is seen arriving with his satchel
and being presented with a hornbook by Nicostrata, the Latin
muse Carmentis, who changed the Greek alphabet into the
Latin. She admits him by the key of *congruitas* to the House
of Wisdom ("Wisdom hath builded her house, she hath hewn
out her seven pillars," *Proverbs* ix. 1). In the lowest story he
begins his course in Donatus under a Bachelor of Arts armed
with the birch; in the next he is promoted to Priscian. Then
follow the other subjects of the *Trivium* and the *Quadrivium*,
each subject being represented by its chief exponent—logic by
Aristotle, arithmetic by Boethius, geometry by Euclid, etc.
Ptolemy, the philosopher, who represents astronomy, is con-
fused with the kings of the same name. Pliny and Seneca
represent the more advanced study of physical and of moral
science respectively, and the edifice is crowned by Theology,
the long and arduous course for which followed that of the
Arts. Its representative in a medieval treatise is naturally
Peter Lombard.

NOTE

I WISH to express my obligations to many recent writers on University history, and to the editors of University Statutes and other records, from which my illustrations of medieval student life have been derived. I owe special gratitude to Dr Hastings Rashdall, Fellow of New College and Canon of Hereford, my indebtedness to whose great work, *The Universities of Europe in the Middle Ages*, is apparent throughout the following pages. Dr Rashdall has been good enough to read my proof-sheets, and to make valuable criticisms and suggestions, and the Master of Emmanuel has rendered me a similar service.

R. S. R.

23rd January 1912.

CONTENTS

CHAPTER I—INTRODUCTORY

CHAPTER II—LIFE IN THE STUDENT-UNIVERSITIES

CHAPTER III—THE UNIVERSITIES OF MASTERS

CHAPTER IV—COLLEGE DISCIPLINE

LIFE IN THE MEDIEVAL UNIVERSITY

CHAPTER I

INTRODUCTORY

" A Clerk ther was of Oxenford also,
That unto logik hadde longe y-go
As lene was his hors as is a rake,
And he was not right fat, I undertake ;
But loked holwe, and therto soberly.
Ful thredbar was his overest courtepy,
For he had geten him yet no benefyce,
Ne was so worldly for to have offyce.
For him was lever have at his beddes heed
Twenty bokes, clad in blak or reed,
Of Aristotle and his philosophye,
Than robes riche, or fithele, or gay sautrye.
But al be that he was a philosophre,
Yet hadde he but litel gold in cofre ;
But al that he might of his freendes hente,
On bokes and on lerninge he it spente,
And bisily gan for the soules preye
Of hem that yaf him wherwith to scoleye,
Of studie took he most cure and most hede,
Noght o word spak he more than was nede,
And that was seyd in forme and reverence
And short and quik, and ful of hy sentence.
Souninge in moral vertu was his speche.
And gladly wolde he lerne, and gladly teche."

AN account of life in the medieval University
might well take the form of a commentary upon the
classical description of a medieval English student.
His dress, the character of his studies and the nature
of his materials, the hardships and the natural
ambitions of his scholar's life, his obligations to
founders and benefactors, suggest learned expositions
which might

> in judicious hands
> Extend from here to Mesopotamy,

and will serve for a modest attempt to picture the
environment of one of the Canterbury pilgrims.

Chaucer's famous lines do more than afford opportunities of explanation and comment ; they give
us an indication of the place assigned to universities
and their students by English public opinion in the
later Middle Ages. The monk of the " Prologue "
is simply a country gentleman. No accusation of
immorality is brought against him, but he is a
jovial huntsman who likes the sound of the bridle
jingling in the wind better than the call of the
church bells, a lover of dogs and horses, of rich
clothes and great feasts. The portrait of the friar
is still less sympathetic ; he is a frequenter of
taverns, a devourer of widows' houses, a man of
gross, perhaps of evil, life. The monk abandons
his cloister and its rules, the friar despises the poor

and the leper. The poet is making no socialistic
attack upon the foundations of society, and no
heretical onslaught upon the Church ; he draws a
portrait of two types of the English regular clergy.
His description of two types of the English secular
clergy forms an illuminating contrast. The noble
verses, in which he tells of the virtues of the parish
priest, certainly imply that the seculars also had their
temptations and that they did not always resist
them ; but the fact remains that Chaucer chose as
the representative of the parochial clergy one who

> " wayted after no pompe and reverence,
> Ne maked him a spyced conscience,
> But Cristes lore, and his apostles twelve,
> He taughte, but first he folwed it himselve."

The history of pious and charitable foundations is
a vindication of the truth of the portraiture of the
" Prologue." The foundation of a new monastery
and the endowment of the friars had alike ceased
to attract the benevolent donor, who was turning
his attention to the universities, where secular
clergy were numerous. The clerks of Oxford and
Cambridge had succeeded to the place held by the
monks, and, after them, by the friars, in the affection
and the respect of the nation.

Outside the kingdom of England the fourteenth
century was also a great period in the growth of

universities and colleges, to which, all over Europe, privileges and endowments were granted by popes, emperors, kings, princes, bishops and municipalities. To attempt to indicate the various causes and conditions which, in different countries, led to the growth, in numbers and in wealth, of institutions for the pursuit of learning would be to wander from our special topic ; but we may take the period from the middle of the fourteenth to the middle of the fifteenth century as that in which the medieval University made its greatest appeal to the imagination of the peoples of Europe.   Its institutional forms had become definite, its terminology fixed, and the materials for a study of the life of the fourteenth century student are abundant.   The conditions of student life varied, of course, with country and climate, and with the differences in the constitutions of individual universities and in their relations to Church and State.   No single picture of the medieval student can be drawn, but it will be convenient to choose the second half of the fourteenth century, or the first half of the fifteenth, as the central point of our investigation.

We have already used technical terms, " University," " College," " Student," which require elucidation, and others will arise in the course of our inquiry. What is a University ?   At the present day a University is, in England, a corporation whose power of granting certain degrees is recognised by the State ; but nothing of this is implied in the word "University." Its literal meaning is simply an association. Recent writers on University history have pointed out that *Universitas vestra*, in a letter addressed to a body of persons, means merely " the whole of you " and that the term was by no means restricted to learned bodies. It was frequently applied to municipal corporations ; Dr Rashdall, in his learned work, tells us that it is used by medieval writers in addressing " all faithful Christian people," and he quotes an instance in which Pisan captives at Genoa in the end of the thirteenth century formed themselves into a "Universitas carcera- torum." The word "College" affords us no further enlightenment. It, too, means literally a community or association, and, unlike the sister term University, it has never become restricted to a scholastic association. The Senators of the "College of Justice" are the judges of the Supreme Court in Scotland.

We must call in a third term to help us. In what we should describe as the early days of European universities, there came into use a phrase some- times written as *Studium Universale* or *Studium Commune*, but more usually *Studium Generale*. It was used in much the same sense in which we speak of a University to-day, and a short sketch of its history is necessary for the solution of our problem.

The twelfth century produced in Europe a renewal of interest and a revival of learning, brought about partly by the influence of great thinkers like St Anselm and Abelard, and partly by the discovery of lost works of Aristotle. The impulse thus given to study resulted in an increase in the numbers of students, and students were naturally attracted to schools where masters and teachers possessed, or had left behind them, great names. At Bologna there was a great teacher of the Civil Law in the first quarter of the twelfth century, and a great writer on Canon Law lived there in the middle of the same century. To Bologna, therefore, there flocked students of law, though not of law alone. In the schools of Paris there were great masters of philosophy and theology to whom students crowded from all parts of Europe. Many of the foreign students at Paris were Englishmen, and when, at the time of Becket's quarrel with Henry II., the disputes between the sovereigns of England and France led to the recall of English students from the domain of their King's enemy, there grew up at Oxford a great school or Studium, which acquired something of the fame of Paris and Bologna. A struggle between the clerks who studied at Oxford and the people of the town broke out at the time of John's defiance of the Papacy, when the King outlawed the clergy of England, and this struggle led to the rise of a school at Cambridge. In Italy the institutions of the Studium at Bologna were copied at Modena, at Reggio, at Vicenza, at Arezzo, at Padua, and elsewhere, and in 1244 or 1245 Pope Innocent IV. founded a Studium of a different constitution, in dependence upon the Papal Court. In Spain great schools grew up at Palencia, Salamanca, and Valladolid; in France at Montpellier, Orleans, Angers, and Toulouse, and at Lyons and Reims. The impulse given by Bologna and Paris was thus leading to the foundation of new Studia or the development of old ones, for there were schools of repute at many of the places we have mentioned before the period with which we are now dealing (c. 1170-1250). It was inevitable that there should be a rivalry among these numerous schools, a rivalry which was accentuated as small and insignificant Studia came to claim for themselves equality of status with their older and greater contemporaries. Thus, in the latter half of the thirteenth century, there arose a necessity for a definition and a restriction of the term Studium Generale. The desirability of a definition was enhanced by the practice of granting to ecclesiastics dispensations from residence in their benefices for purposes of study; to prevent abuses it was essential that such permission should be limited to a number of recognised Studia Generalia.

The difficulty of enforcing such a definition throughout almost the whole of Europe might seem likely to be great, but in point of fact it was inconsiderable. In the first half of the thirteenth century, the term Studium Generale was assuming a recognised significance ; a school which aspired to the name must not be restricted to natives of a particular town or country, it must have a number of masters, and it must teach not only the Seven Liberal Arts (of which we shall have to speak later), but also one or more of the higher studies of Theology, Law and Medicine (*cf.* Rashdall, vol. i. p. 9). But the title might still be adopted at will by ambitious schools, and the intervention of the great potentates of Europe was required to provide a mechanism for the differentiation of General from Particular Studia. Already, in the twelfth century, an Emperor and a Pope had given special privileges to students at Bologna and other Lombard towns, and a King of France had conferred privileges upon the scholars of Paris. In 1224 the Studium Generale of Naples was founded by the Emperor Frederick II., and in 1231 he gave a great privilege to the School of Medicine at Salerno, a Studium which was much more ancient than Bologna, but which existed solely for the study of Medicine

and exerted no influence upon the growth of the
European universities. Pope Gregory IX. founded
the Studium at Toulouse some fifteen years before
Innocent IV. established the Studium of the Roman
Court. In 1254 Alfonso the Wise of Castile founded
the Studium Generale of Salamanca. Thus it
became usual for a school which claimed the status
of a Studium Generale to possess the authority of
Pope or Emperor or King.

A distinction gradually arose between a Studium
Generale under the authority of a Pope or an Emperor and one which was founded by a King or a
City Republic, and which was known as a *Studium
Generale respectu regni*. The distinction was founded
upon the power of the Emperor or the Pope to grant
the *jus ubique docendi*. This privilege, which could
be conferred by no lesser potentate, gave a master
in one Studium Generale the right of teaching in
any other ; it was more valuable in theory than in
practice, but it was held in such esteem that in 1292
Bologna and Paris accepted the privilege from Pope
Nicholas IV. Some of the Studia which we have
mentioned as existing in the first half of the thirteenth
century—Modena in Italy, and Lyons and Reims
in France—never obtained this privilege, and as
their organisation and their importance did not
justify their inclusion among Studia Generalia,
they never took rank among the universities of

Europe.   The status of Bologna and of Paris was, of course, universally recognised before and apart from the Bulls of Nicholas IV.; Padua did not accept a Papal grant until 1346 and then merely as a confirmation, not a creation, of its privileges as a Studium Generale ; Oxford never received, though it twice asked for, a declaratory or confirmatory Bull, and based its claim upon immemorial custom and its own great position.   Cambridge, which in the thirteenth century was a much less important seat of learning than Oxford, was formally recognised as a Studium Generale by Pope John XXII. in 1318 ; but its claim to the title had long been admitted, at all events within the realm of England.   After 1318 Cambridge could grant the *licentia ubique docendi*, which Oxford did not formally confer, although Oxford men, as the graduates of a Studium Generale, certainly possessed the privilege.

Long before the definition of a Studium Generale as a school possessing, by the gift of Pope or Emperor, the *jus ubique docendi*, was generally accepted throughout Europe, we find the occurrence of the more familiar term, " Universitas," which we are now in a position to understand.

A Universitas was an association in the world of learning which corresponded to a Guild in the world of commerce, a union among men living in a Studium and possessing some common interests to protect and advance. Originally, a Universitas could exist in a less important school than a Studium Generale, but with exceptional instances of this kind we are not concerned. By the time which we have chosen for the central point of our survey, the importance of these guilds or Universitates had so greatly increased that the word "Universitas" was coming to be equivalent to "Studium Generale." In the fifteenth century, Dr Rashdall tells us, the two terms were synonymous. The Universitas Studii, the guild of the School, became, technically and officially, the Studium Generale itself, and Studia Generalia were distinguished by the kind of Universitates or guilds which they possessed. It is usual to speak of Bologna and Paris as the two great archetypal universities, and this description does not depend upon mere priority of date or upon the impetus given to thought and interest in Europe by their teachers or their methods. Bologna and Paris were two Studia Generalia with two different and irreconcilable types of Universitas. The Universitates of the Studium of Bologna were guilds of students ; the Universitas of the Studium of Paris was a guild of masters. The great seats of learning in Medieval Europe were either universities of students or universities of masters, imitations of Bologna or of Paris, or modifications of one or the other or of both. It would be impossible to draw up a list and divide medieval universities into compartments. Nothing is more difficult to classify than the constitutions of living societies ; a constitution which one man might regard as a modification of the constitution of Bologna would be in the opinion of another more correctly described as a modification of the constitution of Paris, and a development in the constitution of a University might be held to have altered its fundamental position and to transfer it from one class to another.

Where students legislated for themselves, their rules were neither numerous nor detailed. Our information about life in the student-universities is, therefore, comparatively small, and it is with the universities of masters that we shall be chiefly concerned. It is, however, essential to understand the powers acquired by the student-guilds at Bologna, the institutions of which were reproduced by most of the Italian universities, by those of Spain and Portugal, and, much less accurately, by the smaller universities of France.

CHAPTER II

THE Universitates or guilds which were formed in the Studium Generale of Bologna were associations of foreign students. The lack of political unity in the Italian peninsula was one of the circumstances that led to the peculiar and characteristic constitution evolved by the Italian universities. A famous Studium in an Italian city state must of necessity attract a large proportion of foreign students. These foreign students had neither civil nor political rights ; they were men " out of their own law," for whom the government under which they lived made small and uncertain provision. Their strength lay in their numbers, and in the effect which their presence produced upon the prosperity and the reputation of the town. They early recognised the necessity of union if full use was to be made of the offensive and defensive weapons they possessed. The men who came to study law at Bologna were not schoolboys ; some of them were beneficed ecclesiastics, others were lawyers, and most of them were possessed of adequate means of living. The provisions of Roman Law favoured the creation of such protective guilds; the privileges and immunities of the clergy afforded an analogy for the claim of foreign students to possess laws of their own; and the threat of the secession of a large community was likely to render a city state amenable to argument. The growth of guilds or communities held together by common interests and safeguarded by solemn oaths is one of the features of European history of the twelfth and thirteenth centuries, and the students of Bologna took no unusual or extraordinary step when they formed their Universitates.

The distinction of students into "Nations," which is still preserved in some of the Scottish universities, is derived from this guild-forming movement at Bologna at the end of the twelfth and the beginning of the thirteenth century. No citizen of Bologna was permitted to be a member of a guild, the protection of which he did not require. The tendency at first was towards the formation of a number of Universitates, membership of which was decided by considerations of nationality. But the conditions which had led to the formation of these Universitates were also likely to produce some measure of unification, and the law-students at Bologna soon ceased to have more than two great guilds, distinguished on geographical principles as the Universitas Citramontanorum and the Univer-

sitas Ultramontanorum. Each was sub-divided into
nations ; the cis-Alpine University consisting of
Lombards, Tuscans, and Romans, and the trans-
Alpine University of a varying number, including a
Spanish, a Gascon, a Provençal, a Norman, and an
English nation. The three cis-Alpine nations were,
of course, much more populous at Bologna than the
dozen or more trans-Alpine nations, and they were
therefore sub-divided into sections known as Con-
siliariae. The students of Arts and Medicine, who
at first possessed no organisation of their own and
were under the control of the great law-guilds,
succeeded in the fourteenth century in establishing
a new Universitas within the Studium. The influence of Medicine predominated, for the Arts
course was, at Bologna, regarded as merely a preparation for the study of Law and, especially, of
Medicine ; but this third Universitas gave a definite
status and definite rights to the students of Arts.
In the same century the two jurist universities
came to act together so constantly that they were,
for practical purposes, united, so that, by the beginning of the fifteenth century, the Studium Generale
of Bologna contained virtually two universities,
one of Law, and the other of Arts and Medicine,
governed by freely-elected rectors. The peculiar
relations of Theology to the Studium and to
the universities is a topic which belongs to

constitutional history, and not to our special subject.

The universities of Bologna had to maintain a struggle with two other organisations, the guilds of masters and the authorities of the city state. They kept the first in subjection ; they ultimately succumbed to the second. A guild of masters, doctors, or professors had existed in the Studium before the rise of the Universitates, and it survived with limited, but clearly defined, powers. The words " Doctor," " Professor," and " Magister " or " Dominus " were at first used indifferently, and a Master of Arts of a Scottish or a German University is still described on his diploma as a Doctor of Philosophy. The term " Master " was little used at Bologna, but it is convenient to employ " master " and " student " as the general terms for teacher and taught. The masters were the teachers of the Studium, and they protected their own interests by forming a guild the members of which, and they alone, had the right to teach. Graduation was originally admission into the guild of masters, and the chief privilege attached to it was the right to teach. This privilege ultimately became merely a theoretical right at Bologna, where the teachers tended to become a close corporation of professors, like the Senatus of a Scottish University.

The Guild or College of Masters who taught law

in the Studium of Bologna naturally resented the
rise of the universities of students. The doctors,
they said, should elect the rectors, as they do at
Paris. The scholars follow no trade, they are merely
the pupils of those who do practise a profession, and
they have no right to choose rulers for themselves
any more than the apprentices of the skinners. The
masters were citizens of Bologna, and it might be
expected that the State would assist them in their
struggle with a body of foreign apprentices ; but the
threat of migration turned the scales in favour of the
students. There were no buildings and no endowments to render a migration difficult, and migration
did from time to time take place. The masters
themselves were dependent upon fees for their liveli-
hood ; they were, at Bologna, frequently laymen
with no benefice to fall back upon, and with wives
and children to maintain. As time went on and the
teaching masters became a limited number of professors, they were given salaries, at first by the
student-universities themselves and afterwards by
the city, which feared to offend the student-universities. They thus passed, to a large extent, under the
control of the universities ; how far, we shall see
as our story progresses. The city authorities tried
ineffectually to curb the universities and to prevent
migrations, but the students, with the support of
the Papacy, succeeded in maintaining the strength

of their organisations, and when, in the middle of the fourteenth century, secessions from Bologna came to an end, the students had obtained the recognition and most of the privileges they desired. In course of time the authority of the State increased at Bologna and elsewhere, bodies of Reformatores Studii came to be appointed by republics or tyrants in Italian university-cities, and these boards gradually absorbed the government of the universities. The foundation of residential colleges, and the erection of buildings by the universities themselves, deprived the students of the possibility of reviving the long disused weapon of a migration, and when the power of the Papacy became supreme in Bologna, the freedom of its student-universities came to an end. This, however, belongs to a later age. We must now attempt to obtain some picture of the life of a medieval student at Bologna during the greatness of the Universitates.

We will choose an Englishman who arrives at Bologna early in the fifteenth century to study law. He finds himself at once a member of the English nation of the Trans-montane University ; he pays his fee, takes the oath of obedience to the Rector, and his name is placed upon the " matricula " or roll of members of the University. He does not look about for a lodging-house, like a modern student in a Scottish University, but joins with some companions (*socii*) probably of his own nation, to take a house. If our newcomer had been a Spaniard, he might have been fortunate enough to find a place in the great Spanish College which had been founded in the latter half of the fourteenth century ; as it is, he and his friends settle down almost as citizens of Bologna. The success of the universities in their attempt to form a citizenship outside the state had long ago resulted in the creation also of a semi-citizenship within the state. The laws of the city of Bologna allowed the students to be regarded as citizens so long as they were members of a University. Our young Englishman has, of course, no share in the government of the town, but he possesses all rights necessary for the protection of his person and property ; he can make a legal will and bring an action against a citizen. The existence of these privileges, unusual and remarkable in a medieval state, may excite his curiosity about the method by which they were acquired, and he will probably be told strange and terrible tales of the bad old times, when a foreign student was as helpless as any other foreigner in a strange town, and might be tortured by unfair and tyrannous judges. If he is historically minded, he will learn about the rise of the smaller guilds which are now amalgamated in his Universitas ; how, like other guilds, they were benefit societies caring for the sick and the poor, burying the dead, and providing for common religious services and common feasts. He will be told (in language unfamiliar at Oxford) how the proctors or representatives of the guild were sent to cheer up the sick and, if necessary, to relieve their necessities, and to reconcile members who had quarrelled. The corporate payment for feasts included the cost of replacing broken windows, which (at all events among the German students at Bologna) seem to have been associated with occasions of rejoicing. The guild would pay for the release of one of its members who was in prison, but it would also insist upon the payment of the debts, even of those who had " gone down." It was essential that the credit of the guild with the citizens of Bologna should be maintained.

Many of these purposes were still served by the " nation " to which our Bologna freshman belonged : but the really important organisation was that of his Universitas. One of his first duties might happen to be connected with the election of a new Rector. The title of the office was common in Italy and was the equivalent of the Podesta, or chief magistrate, of an Italian town. The choice of a new Rector would probably be limited, for the honour was costly, and the share of the fines which the Rector received could not nearly meet his expenses. As his jurisdiction included clerks, it was necessary, by the Canon Law, that he should have the tonsure, and be, at all events technically, a clerk. He could not belong to any religious order, his obligations to which might conflict with his duty to the Universitas, and the expense of the office made it desirable that he should be a beneficed clergyman who was dispensed from residence in his benefice ; he could enter upon his duties at the age of twenty-four, and he was not necessarily a priest or even a deacon. Our freshman played a small part in the election. As a member of the English nation, he would help to choose a Consiliarius, who had a vote in the election, and who became one of the Rector's permanent Council. The dignity of the Rector's position would be impressed upon our novice by his senior contemporaries, who could boast that, if a Cardinal came to Bologna, he must yield precedence to the Rector, and the lesson would be emphasised by a great feast on the occasion of the solemn installation and possibly by a tournament and a dance, certainly by some more magnificent banquet than that given by a Rector of the University of Arts and Medicine. After our student's day there grew up a strange ceremony of tearing the robe of the new Rector and selling back the pieces to him, and statutes had to be passed prohibiting the acceptance of money for the fragments, although if any student succeeded in capturing the robe without injuring it, he might claim its redemption. The state and hospitality which the office entailed led to its being made compulsory to accept the offer of it, but this arrangement failed to maintain the ancient prestige of the Rectorship which, after the decline of the Universitates themselves, had outlived its usefulness.

Magnificent as was the position of the Rector of a Universitas, our young Englishman would soon discover that his Rector was only a constitutional sovereign. He had to observe the statutes and to consult his Council upon important questions. He had no power to dispense with the penalties imposed by the regulations, and for any mismanagement of the pecuniary affairs of the Universitas he was personally liable, when at the end of his period of office he had to meet a Committee and to render an account of his stewardship. He could sentence offending students to money fines, but he must have the consent of his Council before expelling them or declaring them subject to the ecclesiastical and social penalties of the perjured man. He claimed to try cases brought by students against townsmen, and about the time of our scholar's arrival, the town had admitted that he might try students accused of criminal offences forbidden by the University statutes, and had agreed to carry out his sentences. Too free a use of the secular arm would naturally

lead to unpopularity and trouble ; the spectacle of
a student being handed over to the gaolers of the
Podesta or of the Bishop can never have been
pleasant in the eyes of a Universitas. Changes in
the statutes of the University could not be made by
the Rector ; every twenty years eight " Statutarii "
were appointed to revise the code, and alterations
made at other times required the consent of the
Congregation, which consisted of all students except
citizens of Bologna and a few poor scholars who did
not subscribe to the funds of the Universitas.   By
the time of which we are speaking, the two jurist-
universities at Bologna met together in one Congregation, and if a Congregation happens to be held
during our Englishman's residence at Bologna,
he will find himself bound under serious penalties
to attend its session, where he will mix on equal
terms with members of the Cismontane University,
listening to, or taking part in, the debates (conducted
in Latin) and throwing his black or white bean into
the ballot box when a vote is necessary.

Although the city of Bologna never admitted the
jurisdiction of a Universitas over citizens of the
town, there were some classes of citizens whose trade
or profession made them virtually its subjects.
Landlords, stationers, and masters or doctors were
in a peculiar relation to the universities, which did
not fail to use their advantage to the uttermost.

If our English student and his *socii* had any dispute about the rent of their house, there was a compulsory system of arbitration ; if he found an error in a MS. which he had hired or purchased from a Bologna bookseller he was bound to report it to a University Board whose duty it was to inspect MSS. offered for sale or hire, and the bookseller would be ordered to pay a fine ; he was protected from extortionate prices by a system which allowed the bookseller a fixed profit on a second-hand book. MSS. were freely reproduced by the booksellers' clerks, and were neither scarce nor unduly expensive, although elaborately illuminated MSS. were naturally very valuable. The landlords and the booksellers were kept in proper submission by threats of *interdictio* or *privatio*. A citizen who offended the University was debarred from all intercourse with students, who were strictly forbidden to hire his house or his books ; if a townsman brought a " calumnious accusation " against a student, and disobeyed a rectorial command to desist, he and his children, to the third generation, and all their goods, were to lie under an interdict, " *sine spe restitutionis.*"

Interdictio, or discommuning, was also the great weapon which might be employed against the masters of the Studium. The degradation of the masters was a gradual process, and it was never complete. The privileges given by Frederick Barbarossa to Lombard scholars in the middle of the twelfth century included a right of jurisdiction over their pupils, and a Papal Bull of the end of the century speaks of masters and scholars meeting together in congregations. The organisation of the Universitas ultimately confined membership of congregation to students, and the powers of the Rector rendered the magisterial jurisdiction merely nominal. The loss of their privileges is attributed by Canon Rashdall to the attitude they adopted in the early struggles between the municipality and the student-guilds. The doctors, who were citizens of Bologna, allied themselves, he says, " with the City against the students in the selfish effort to exclude from the substantial privileges of the Doctorate all but their own fellow-citizens. . . . It was through identifying themselves with the City rather than with the scholars that the Doctors of Bologna sank into their strange and undignified servitude to their own pupils." They made a further mistake in quarrelling with the town —the earliest migrations were migrations of professors—and when, in the middle of the thirteenth century, a permanent *modus vivendi* was arrived at between the city and the universities, the rights of the doctors received no consideration. Other citizens of Bologna were forbidden to take an oath of obedience to the rectors, but the masters, who, in theory, possessed rights of jurisdiction over their pupils, were, in fact, compelled by the universities to take this oath.   Even those of them who received salaries from the town were not exempted. A doctor who refused to take a vow of obedience to the representative of his pupils had no means of collecting his lecture-fees, which remained of some importance even after the introduction of salaries, and he was liable to further punishment at the will of the Rector.   The ultimate penalty was *deprivatio*, and when this sentence was pronounced, not only were the lectures of the offending doctor boycotted, but all social intercourse with him was forbidden ; students must avoid his company in private as well as decline his ministrations in the Studium.   His restoration could only be accomplished by a vote of the whole University solemnly assembled in Congregation.

The oath of obedience was not merely a constitutional weapon kept in reserve for occasional serious disputes ; it affected the daily life of the Studium, and the masters were subject to numerous petty indignities, which could not fail to impress our English student if he was familiar with University life in his own country.   He would see, with surprise, a doctor's lecture interrupted by the arrival of a University Bedel, as the debates of the House of Commons are interrupted by the arrival of Black Rod, and his instructor would maintain a reverent silence while the Rector's officer delivered some message from the University, or informed the professor of some new regulation. If the learned doctor " cut " a lecture, our student would find himself compelled to inform the authorities of the University, and he would hear of fines inflicted upon the doctors for absence, for lateness, for attracting too small an audience, for omitting portions of a subject or avoiding the elucidation of its difficulties, and for inattention while the " precepta " or " mandata " of the Rector were being read in the schools.   He and his fellow-students might graciously grant their master a holiday, but the permission had to be confirmed by the Rector ; if a lecture was prolonged a minute after the appointed time, the doctor found himself addressing empty benches. The humiliation of the master's position was increased by the fact that his pupils were always acting as spies upon him, and they were themselves liable to penalties for conniving at any infringement of the regulations on his part.   At Bologna, even the privilege of teaching was, to a slight extent, shared by the doctors with their pupils.   Lectures were divided into two classes, ordinary and extra-ordinary ; the ordinary lectures were the duty of the doctors, but senior students (bachelors) were authorised by the Rector to share with the doctors the duty of giving extra-ordinary lectures.   There

were six chairs, endowed by the city, which were
held by students, and the occupant of one of these
was entitled to deliver ordinary lectures. Dr
Rashdall finds the explanation of this anomaly in
an incident in the fourteenth century history of
Bologna, when the Tyrant of the City forbade the
professors to teach. The student-chairs were rather
endowments for the Rectorship or for poor scholars
than serious rivals to the ordinary professorships,
and the extra-ordinary lectures delivered by students
or bachelors may be regarded as a kind of apprenticeship for future doctors.

There remained one department of the work of
the Studium in which our Bologna student would
find his masters supreme. The sacred right of
examining still belonged to the teachers, even
though the essential purpose of the examination was
changed. The doctors of Bologna had succeeded
in preserving the right to teach as a privilege of
Bolognese citizens and even of restricting it, to some
extent, to certain families, and the foreign student
could not hope to become a professor of his own
studium. But the prestige of the University
rendered Bolognese students ambitious of the
doctorate, and the doctorate had come to mean
more than a mere licence to teach. This licence,
which had originally been conferred by the doctors
themselves, required, after the issue of a Papal

Bull in 1219, the consent of the Archdeacon of Bologna, and the Papal grant of the *jus ubique docendi* in 1292 increased at once the importance of the mastership and of the authority of the Archdeacon, who came to be described as the Chancellor and Head of the Studium. " Graduation," in Dr Rashdall's words, " ceased to imply the mere admission into a private Society of teachers, and bestowed a definite legal status in the eyes of Church and State alike. . . . The Universities passed from merely local into ecumenical organisations ; the Doctorate became an order of intellectual nobility with as distinct and definite a place in the hierarchical system of medieval Christendom as the Priesthood or the Knighthood." The Archdeacon of Bologna, even when he was regarded as the Chancellor, did not wrest from the college of doctors the right to decide who should be deemed worthy of a title which Cardinals were pleased to possess. The licence which he required before admitting a student to the doctorate continued to be conferred by the Bologna doctors after due examination.

We will assume that our English student has now completed his course of study. He has duly attended the prescribed lectures—not less than three a week. He has gone in the early mornings, when the bell at St Peter's Church was ringing for mass, to spend some two hours listening to the " ordinary " lecture delivered by a doctor in his own house or in a hired room ; his successors a generation or two later would find buildings erected by the University for the purpose. The rest of his morning and an hour or two in the afternoon have also, if he is an industrious student, been devoted to lectures, and he has not been neglectful of private study. He has enjoyed the numerous holidays afforded by the Feasts of the Church, and several vacations in the course of the year, including ten days at Christmas, a fortnight at Easter, and about six weeks in the autumn. After five years of study, if he is a civilian, and four if he is a canonist, the Rector has raised him to the dignity of a Bachelor by permitting him to give " extra-ordinary " lectures—and after two more years spent in this capacity he is ready to proceed to the doctorate. The Rector, having been satisfied by the English representative in his Council that the " doctorand " has performed the whole duty of the Bolognese student, gives him permission to enter for the first or Private Examination, and he again takes the oath of obedience to that dignitary. The doctor under whom he has studied vouches for his competence, and presents him first to the Archdeacon and some days afterwards to the College of Doctors, before whom he takes a solemn oath never to seek admittance into the Bolognese College of Doctors, or to teach, or attempt to perform any of the functions of a doctor, at Bologna. They then give him a passage for exposition and send him home. He is followed to his house by his own doctor who hears his exposition in private, and brings him back to the august presence of the College of Doctors and the Archdeacon. Here he treats his thesis and is examined upon it by two or more doctors, who are ordered by the University statutes not to treat any victim of this rigorous and tremendous examination otherwise than if he were their own son, and are threatened with grave penalties, including suspension for a year. The College then votes upon his case, each doctor saying openly and clearly, and without any qualification, " Approbo " or " Reprobo," and if the decision is favourable he is now a Licentiate and has to face only the expensive but not otherwise formidable ordeal of the second or Public Examination. As a newly appointed Scottish judge is, to this day, admitted to his office by trying cases, so the Bologna doctor was admitted to his new dignity by an exercise in lecturing. The idea is common to many medieval institutions, and it survived at Bologna, even though the licentiate had, at his private examination, renounced the right of teaching. Our Englishman and his socii go together to the Cathedral, where he states a thesis and defends it against the attacks of other licentiates. His own doctor, known in Bologna (and elsewhere) as the Promotor, presents him to the Chancellor, who confers upon him the *jus ubique docendi*. He is then seated in a master's chair, and the Promotor gives him an open book and a gold ring and (in the terminology of a modern Scottish University) " caps " him with the biretta.   He is dismissed with a benediction and the kiss of peace, and is conducted through the town, in triumphal procession, by his friends, to whom he gives a feast.

The feast adds very considerably to the expenses of the doctorate, for which fees are, of course, exacted by the authorities of the University, the College of Doctors, and the Archdeacon. A considerable proportion of the disciplinary regulations, made by the student-universities, aimed at restricting the expenditure on feasting at the inception of a new doctor and on other occasions. When our young English Doctorand received the permission of his Rector to proceed to his degree, he was made to promise not to exceed the proper expenditure on fees and feasts, and he was expressly forbidden to organise a tournament. The spending of money on extravagant costume was also prohibited by the statutes of the University, which forbade a student to purchase, either directly or through an agent, any costume other than the ordinary black garment, or any outer covering other than the black cappa or gabard. Other disciplinary restrictions at Bologna dealt with quarrelling and gambling. The debates of Congregation were not to be liable to interruption by one student stabbing his opponent in Italian fashion, and no one was allowed to carry arms to a meeting of Congregation ; if a student had reason to apprehend personal violence from another, the Rector could give him a dispensation from the necessity of attendance. Gaming and borrowing from unauthorised money-lenders were strictly forbidden ; to enter a gaming-house, or to keep one, or to watch a game of dice was strictly forbidden. The University of Arts and Medicine granted a dispensation for three days at Christmas, and a Rector might use his own discretion in the matter. The penalties were fines, and for contumacy or grave offences, suspension or expulsion.

There are indications that the conduct of the doctors in these respects was not above suspicion ; they were expressly prohibited from keeping gaming-houses ; and the appointment of four merchants of the town, who alone were empowered to lend money to students, was a protection not only against ordinary usurers, but also against doctors who lent money to students in order to attract them to their lectures. That the ignominious position of the Bologna doctors had an evil effect upon their morals, is evident not only from this, but also from

C

the existence of bribery, in connection with examinations for the doctorate, although corruption of this kind was not confined to the student-universities.

The regulations of the greatest of the residential colleges of Bologna, the College of Spain, naturally interfere much more with individual liberty than do the statutes of the student-universities, even though the government of the College was a democracy, based upon the democratic constitution of the University. We shall have an opportunity of referring to the discipline of the Spanish College when we deal with the College system in the northern universities, and meanwhile we pass to some illustrations of life in student-universities elsewhere than at Bologna.

At Padua we find a " Schools-peace " like the special peace of the highway or the market in medieval England ; special penalties were prescribed for attacks on scholars in the Schools, or going to or returning from the Schools at the accustomed hours. The presence of the Rector also made a slight attack count as an " atrocious injury." The University threatened to interdict, for ten years, the ten houses nearest to the place where a scholar was killed ; if he was wounded the period was four or six years. At Florence, where the Faculty of Medicine was very important, there is an interesting provision for the study of anatomy.

An agreement was made with the town, by which the students of Medicine were to have two corpses every year, one male and one female. The bodies were to be those of malefactors, who gained, to some extent, by the arrangement, for the woman's penalty was to be changed from burning, and the man's from decapitation, to hanging. A pathetic clause provides that the criminals are not to be natives of Florence, but of captive race, with few friends or relations. If the number of medical students increased, they were to have two male bodies. At Florence, as almost everywhere, we find regulations against gambling, but an exception was made for the Kalends of May and the days immediately before and after, and no penalty could be inflicted for gambling in the house of the Rector. The records of Florence afford an illustration of the checks upon the rectorial power, to which we have referred in speaking of the typical Student-University at Bologna. In 1433, a series of complaints were brought against a certain Hieronimus who had just completed his year of office as Rector, and a Syndicate, consisting of a Doctor of Decrees (who was also a scholar in civil law), a scholar in Canon Law, and a scholar in Medicine, was appointed to inquire into the conduct of the late Rector and of his two Camerarii. The accusations were both general and personal, and the Syndics, after deciding

that Hieronimus must restore eight silver *grossi*
of University money which he had appropriated,
proceeded to hear the charges brought by individuals.
A lecturer in the University complained that the
Rector had unjustly and maliciously given a sentence
against him and in favour of a Greek residing at
Florence, and that he had unjustly declared him
perjured ; fifty gold florins were awarded as damages
for this and some other injuries.   A doctor of
Arts and Medicine obtained a judgment for two
florins for expenses incurred when the Rector was
in his house.   A student complained that he had
been denounced as " infamis " in all the Schools
for not paying his matriculation-fee, and that his
name had been entered in the book called the
" Speculum." The Syndics ordered the record of
his punishment to be erased.   The most interesting
case is that of a student of Civil Law, called Andreas
Romuli de Lancisca.   He averred that he had sold
Hieronimus six measures of grain, to be paid for
at the customary price.   After four months' delay,
the Rector paid seven pounds, and when asked to
complete the payment, gave Andreas a book of
medicine, " for which I got five florins." Some days
later he demanded the return of the book, to which
Andreas replied : " Date mihi residuum et libenter
restituam librum." To this request the Rector,
" in superbiam elevatus," answered, " Tu reddes

librum et non solvam tibi." The quarrel continued, and one morning, when Andreas was in the
Schools at a lecture, Hieronimus sent the servant
of the Podesta, who seized him "ignominiose et
vituperose" in the Schools and conducted him to
the town prison like a common thief. For all these
injuries Andreas craved redress and a sum of forty
florins. The damages, he thought, should be high,
not merely for his personal wrongs, but also for the
insult to the scholar's dress which he wore, and,
indeed, to the whole University. He was allowed
twenty pounds in addition to the sum due for the
grain. The Syndicate of 1433 must have been an
extreme case ; matters were complicated by the fact
that the Rector's brother was "Executor Ordina-
mentorum Justitiæ Civitatis Florentiæ," and he was
therefore suspected of playing into the hands of the
city. But the knowledge that such an investigation
was possible must have restrained the arbitrary
tendencies of a Rector.

A reference to the imitation of the Bolognese
constitution in Spain must close this portion of our
survey. At Lerida, in the earliest code of statutes
(about 1300), we find the doctors and master sworn
to obey the Rector, who can fine them, though
he must not expel them without the consent of the
whole University. Any improper criticisms of the
Rector ("verba injuriosa vel contumeliosa") by

anyone, of whatsoever dignity, are to be punished by suspension until satisfaction is made, and so great is the glory of the office (" Rectoris officium tanta [excellentia] præfulget ") that an ex-Rector is not bound to take the oath to his successor. The regulations affecting undergraduates are more detailed than at Bologna, and indicate a stricter discipline. After eight days' attendance at a doctor's lecture, a student must not forsake it to go to another doctor ; no scholar is to go to the School on horseback unless for some urgent cause ; scholars are not to give anything to actors or jesters or other " truffatores " (troubadours), nor to invite them to meals, except on the feasts of Christmas, Easter, and Pentecost, or at the election of a Rector, or when doctors or masters are created. Even on these occasions only food may be given, although an ordinance of the second Rector allows doctors and masters to give them money. No students, except boys under fourteen, are to be allowed to play at ball in the city on St Nicholas' day or St Katherine's day, and none are to indulge in unbecoming amusements, or to walk about dressed up as Jews or Saracens—a rule which is also found in the statutes of the University of Perpignan. If scholars are found bearing arms by day in the students' quarter of the town, they are to forfeit their arms, and if they are found at night with either arms or musical

instruments in the students' quarter, they are to
forfeit arms or instruments. If they are found
outside their own quarters, by night or by day, with
arms or musical instruments, the town officials will
deal with laymen, and the Bishop or the Rector with
clerks. Laymen might be either students or doctors
in Spain as in Italy; at Salamanca, a lecturer's
marriage was included among the necessary causes
which excused a temporary absence from his duties.
In the universities of Southern France, the marriage
of resident doctors and students was also contemplated, and the statutes of the University of Aix
contain a table of charges payable as " charivari "
by a rector, a doctor, a licentiate, a bachelor, a
student, and a bedel. In each case the amount
payable for marrying a widow was double the
ordinary fee. If the bridegroom declined to pay, the
" dominus promotor," accompanied by " dominis
studentibus," was, by permission of the Rector, to
go to his house armed with frying-pans, bassoons,
and horns, and to make a great tumult, without,
however, doing any injury to his neighbours. Continued recusancy was to be punished by placing
filth outside the culprit's door on feast-days. In
the University of Dôle, there was a married Rector
in 1485, but this was by a special dispensation.
There are traces of the existence of married undergraduates at Oxford in the fifteenth century, and,

in the same century, marriage was permitted in the Faculty of Medicine at Paris, but the insistence upon celibacy in the northern universities is one of the characteristic differences between them and the universities of Southern Europe.

CHAPTER III

THE Guild or Universitas which grew up in the Studium Generale of Paris was a Society of masters, not of students. The Studium Generale was, in origin, connected with the Cathedral Schools, and recognition as a Master was granted by the Chancellor of the Cathedral, whose duty it was to confer it upon every competent scholar who asked for it. The successful applicant was admitted by the existing masters into their Society, and this admission or inception was the origin of degrees in the University of Paris. The date of the growth of an organised Guild is uncertain; Dr Rashdall, after a survey of the evidence, concludes that " it is a fairly safe inference that the period 1150-1170 —probably the latter years of that period—saw the birth of the University of Paris." Such organisation as existed in the twelfth century was slight and customary, depending, as the student-universities of Bologna and in other medieval guilds, upon no external authority. The successors of these early masters, writing in the middle of the thirteenth century, relate how their predecessors, men reverend

41

in character and famous for learning, decided, as
the number of their pupils increased, that they
could do their work better if they became a united
body, and that they therefore formed themselves
into a College or University, on which Church and
State conferred many privileges. The bond of
union they describe as a " jus speciale " (" si quodam
essent juris specialis vinculo sociati "), and this
conception explains the appearance of their earliest
code of statutes in the first decade of the thirteenth
century. The Guild of masters at Paris, like the
Guild of students at Bologna, could use with advantage the threat of a migration, and, after a violent
quarrel with the town in the year 1200, they received
special privileges from Philip Augustus. Some years
later, Pope Innocent III. permitted the " scholars
of Paris " to elect a procurator or proctor to represent their interests in law-suits at Rome. Litiga-
tion at Rome was connected with disputes with the
Chancellor of the Cathedral. Already the scholars
of Paris had complained to the Pope about the
tyranny of the Chancellor, and Innocent had sup-
ported their cause, remarking that when he himself
studied at Paris he had never heard of scholars
being treated in this fashion. It moved and aston-
ished the Pope not a little that the Chancellor
should attempt to exact an oath of obedience and
payment of money from the masters, and, in the

end, that official was compelled to give up his claim
to demand fees or oaths of fealty or obedience for a
licence to teach, and to relax any oaths that had
already been taken. The masters, as Dr Rashdall
points out, already possessed the weapon of boy-
cotting, and ordering their students to boycott,
a teacher upon whom the Chancellor conferred a
licence against the wish of their guild, but they
could not at first compel him to grant a licence to
anyone whom they desired to admit. After the
Papal intervention of 1212, the Chancellor was
bound to licence a candidate recommended by the
masters.

In the account of their own history, from which
we have already quoted, the Parisian masters speak
of their venerable " gignasium litterarum " as
divided into four faculties, Theology, Law, Medicine,
and Philosophy, and they compare the four streams
of learning to the four rivers of Paradise. The
largest and most important was the Faculty of Arts,
and the masters of that Faculty were the protagonists
in the struggle with the Chancellor, a struggle which
continued long after the intervention of Innocent III.
In the course of this long and successful conflict,
the Faculty of Arts developed an internal organisation, consisting of four nations, distinguished as the
French, the Normans, the Picards, and the English.
Each nation elected a proctor, and the four proctors

or other representatives of the nations elected a
Rector, who was the Head of the Faculty of Arts.
The division into nations and the title of Rector
may have been copied from Bologna, but the
organisation at Paris was essentially different. The
Parisian nations were governed by masters, not by
students, and whereas, at Bologna, the artists were
an insignificant minority, at Paris, the Rector
became, by the end of the thirteenth century, the
most powerful official of the University, and, by the
middle of the fourteenth, was recognised as its Head.
The superior Faculties of Theology, Canon Law, and
Medicine, though they possessed independent constitutions under their own Deans, consisted largely
of men who had taken a Master's or a Bachelor's
degree in Arts, and, from the middle of the thirteenth
century, they took an oath to the Rector, which was
held to be binding even after they became doctors.
The non-artist members of these Faculties were not
likely to be able to resist an authority whose existence was generally welcomed as the centre of the
opposition to the Chancellor. Ultimately, the whole
University passed under the sway of the Rector,
and the power of the Chancellor was restricted to
granting the *jus ubique docendi* as the representative
of the Pope. Even this was little more than a
formality, for the Chancellor " ceased," says Dr
Rashdall, " to have any real control over the grant

or refusal of Licences, except in so far as he retained the nomination of the Examiners in Arts."

At Oxford, the University was also a Guild of masters, but Oxford was not a cathedral city, and there was no conflict with the Bishop or the Chancellor. In the end of the twelfth or the beginning of the thirteenth century, the masters of the Studium probably elected a Rector or Head in imitation of the Parisian Chancellor. After the quarrel with the citizens, which led to the migration to Cambridge, and when King John had submitted to the Pope, the masters were able to obtain an ordinance from the Papal legate determining the punishment of the offenders, and providing against the recurrence of such incidents. The legate ordered that if the citizens should seize the person of a clerk, his surrender might be demanded by " the Bishop of Lincoln, or the Archdeacon of the place or his Official, or the Chancellor, or whomsoever the Bishop of Lincoln shall depute to this office." The clause lays stress upon the authority of the Bishop of Lincoln, which must in no way be diminished by any action of the townsmen. The ecclesiastical authority of the Bishop was welcomed by the University as a protection against the town, and the Chancellor was too far away from Lincoln to press the privileges of the Diocese or the Cathedral against the clerks who were under his

special care. The Oxford Chancellor was a master of
the Studium, and, though he was the representative
of the Bishop, he was also the Head of the masters'
guild, and from very early times was elected by
the masters. Thus he came to identify himself
with the University, and his office increased in
importance as privileges were conferred upon the
University by kings and popes. No Rectorship
grew up as a rival to the Chancellorship, though
some of the functions of the Parisian Rector were
performed at Oxford by the Proctors. There were
only two "Nations" at Oxford, for the Oxford
masters were, as a rule, Englishmen; men from north
of the Trent formed the Northern Nation, and the
rest of England the Southern Nation. Scotsmen
were classed as Northerners, and Welshmen and
Irishmen as Southerners. The division into Nations
was short-lived, and the two Rectors or Proctors,
though still distinguished as Northern and Southern,
soon became representatives elected by the whole
Faculty of Arts. As at Paris, the Faculty of Arts
was the moving spirit in the University, and Theology, Law, and Medicine never developed at Oxford
any independent organisation. The proctors, as
Dr Rashdall has shown, thus became the Executive
of the University as a whole, and not merely of the
Faculty of Arts.

An essential difference between Bologna and its

two great northern sisters lies in the fact that, at Paris and at Oxford, masters and scholars alike were all clerks, possessing the tonsure and wearing the clerical garb, though not necessarily even in minor orders. They could thus claim the privileges of ecclesiastical jurisdiction, and at Oxford this jurisdiction was exercised by the Chancellor, who also, along with the proctors, was responsible for academic discipline and could settle disputes between members of the University. In this, the University of Oxford had a position of independence which Paris never achieved, for though the Parisian Rector's court dealt with cases of discipline and with internal disputes, criminal jurisdiction remained the prerogative of the Bishop. In the middle of the fourteenth century, royal grants of privileges to the University of Oxford culminated in the subjection of the city, and from the middle of the fifteenth " the burghers lived in their own town almost as the helots or subjects of a conquering people." (*Cf.* Rashdall, vol. ii. chap. 12, sec. 3). The constitution of Oxford was closely imitated at Cambridge, where the Head of the University was also the Chancellor, and the executive consisted of two rectors or proctors. In the fifteenth century the University freed itself from the ecclesiastical jurisdiction of the Bishop of Ely.

Germany possessed no universities before the

fourteenth century. Prague was founded in 1347-8, and was followed before 1400 by Vienna, Erfurt, Heidelberg, and Cologne, and in the first quarter of the next century by Würzburg, Leipsic, Rostock, and in the Low Countries by Louvain. The first Scottish University dates from the early years of the fifteenth century. While the provincial universities of France tended to follow Bologna rather than Paris as their model, the German universities approximated to the Parisian type, and although the founders of the Scottish universities were impressed by some of the conditions of the student-universities, and provided for them a theoretical place in their constitutions, yet the three medieval Scottish universities of Scotland, in their actual working, more nearly resembled the master type.

CHAPTER IV

COLLEGE DISCIPLINE

WE are now in a position to approach the main part
of our subject—life in a medieval University of
masters—and we propose to proceed at once to its
most characteristic feature, life in a medieval
College. The system originated in Paris. In the
early days of the University, students at Paris
lived freely in private houses, which a number of
" socii " hired for themselves. A record of a
dispute which occurred in 1336 shows that it was
usual for one member of such a community to be
responsible for the rent, " tanquam principalis dictae
domus," and the member who was held to be responsible in the particular case is described as a
" magister." At first it was not necessary that he
should be a master, but this soon became usual,
and ultimately (though not till the close of the
Middle Ages) it was made compulsory by the University. Dr Rashdall has drawn attention to the
democratic character of these Hospicia or Halls,
the members of which elected their own principal
and made the regulations which he enforced. This
democratic constitution is found at Oxford as well

as at Paris, and was, indeed, common to all the early universities. When a benevolent donor endowed one of these halls, he invariably gave it not only money, but regulations, and it was the existence of an endowment and of statutes imposed by an external authority that differentiated the College from the Hall. The earliest College founders did not necessarily erect any buildings for the scholars for whose welfare they provided; a College is essentially a society, and not a building. The quadrangular shape which is now associated with the buildings of a College was probably suggested accidentally by the development of Walter de Merton's College at Oxford; but, long after the foundation of Merton College in 1263 or 1264, it was not considered necessary by a founder to build a home for his scholars, who secured a suitable lodging-house (or houses) and were prepared to migrate should such a step become desirable in the interest of the University.

The statutes of Merton provide us with a picture of an endowed Hall at the period when such endowments were beginning to change the character of University life. The conception of a College, as distinguished from the older Halls, developed very rapidly, and the Founder's provisions for the organisation of his society were altered three times within ten years. In 1264, Walter de Merton, sometime

Chancellor of England, drew up a code of statutes for the foundation of a house, to be called the House of the Scholars of Merton. His motive was the good of Holy Church and the safety of the souls of his benefactors and relations, and these objects were to be served by providing for the maintenance of twenty poor scholars and two or three priests in the schools of Oxford, or elsewhere, if learning should, in these days of civil war, flourish elsewhere than at Oxford. The endowment which he provided was to consist of his manors of Maldon and Farleigh, in Surrey, to which was added the Merton estate, at the end of what are now the "Backs" in Cambridge. This was purchased in 1269-70. The lands were given to his scholars, to be held under certain conditions, in their own name. His own kindred were to have the first claim upon places in the new Society, and, after them, natives of the diocese of Winchester; they were to have allowances of forty shillings each per annum, to live together in a Hall, and to wear uniform garb in token of unity and mutual love. As vacancies arose, by death, by admission into a religious order, by the acceptance of livings in the Church, or by appointments in other callings, they were to be filled up, and if the funds of the society permitted, the numbers, both of scholars and of priests, were to be increased. Scholars who proved to be incorrigibly idle, or who led evil lives, were to be deprived ; but the sick and infirm were to be treated generously, and any of the Founder's kin who suffered from an incurable malady, and were incapable of earning an honest living in the Studium or elsewhere, were to be maintained till their death. It was assumed that the scholars had already received the preliminary training in Latin which was necessary for their studies, but provision was made for the elementary instruction of poor or orphan boys of the Founder's kin, until they were ready to enter the University. Once or twice a year all the members of the foundation were to meet and say mass for their Founder and his benefactors, living and dead. The management of the property was entrusted to a Warden, who was to reside not at Oxford or any other Studium where the Hall might happen to be, but at Maldon or Farleigh. The Warden was a member of the Society, but had no authority over the scholars, except that, in cases of disputed elections, he, or the Chancellor or Rector of the University where the Hall happened to be at the time, was to act on the advice of six or seven of the senior scholars, and the senior scholars, rather than the Warden, were looked upon by the founder as the natural leaders of his Society. Every year, eight or ten of the seniors were to go to Surrey to stay for eight days to inquire into the management of their property, and, if at any other time, evil rumours about the conduct of the Warden reached the Hall, two or three of them were to go to investigate. The scholars could, with the consent of the Patron, the Bishop of Winchester, bring about the deposition of the Warden, and elections to the Wardenship were entrusted to the twelve seniors. They were to consult the " brothers " who assisted the Warden at Merton, and were also to obtain the sanction of the Bishop of Winchester.

These first Merton statutes clearly contemplate an endowed Hall, differing from other Halls only in the existence of the endowment. Some regulations are necessary in order that the tenure of the property of the Society may be secure and that its funds may not be misapplied, and the brief code of statutes is directed to these ends. Walter de Merton's earliest rules make the minimum of change in existing conditions. But the preparation of this code of statutes must have suggested to the Founder that his generosity gave him the power of making more elaborate provisions. The Mendicant Orders had already established at Oxford and at Paris houses for their own members, and the Monastic Orders in France were following the example of the Friars. These houses were, of course, governed by minute and detailed regulations, and it may have seemed desirable to introduce some stricter discipline into the secular halls. At all events, in 1270, Walter de Merton took the opportunity of an increase in his endowments to issue a code of statutes more than twice as long as that of 1264. These new statutes mark a distinct advance in the Founder's ideal of College life. The Warden becomes a much more important factor in the conduct of the Hall as well as in the management of the property ; in the election and in the expulsion of scholars he is given a greater place ; his allowances are increased, and his presence at Oxford seems to be implied. The scholars are to proceed from Arts to Theology ; four or five of them may be permitted to study the Canon Law, and the Warden may allow some of them to devote some time to the Civil Law. Two Sub-Wardens are to be appointed, one at Maldon and one in Oxford ; Deans are to watch over the morals of the scholars, and senior students are to preside over the studies of the freshmen. The scholars are to be silent at meals and to listen to a reader ; there must be no noise in their chambers, and a senior is to be in authority in each chamber, and to report breaches of regulations. Conversation is to be conducted in Latin.

We have here the beginnings of a new system of University life, and we can trace the tendency towards collegiate discipline still more clearly in the Founder's statutes of 1274, which are much longer

and more elaborate than in 1270. The scholars or
Fellows are now to obey the Warden, as their
Superior ; the Deans and the seniors in chambers
are to bear rule under him and, in the first instance,
to report to him ; the Sub-Warden is to take his
place in his absence and to assist him at other
times ; three Bursars are to help him in the management of the property. The Patron or Visitor may
inquire into the conduct of the Warden or into any
accusations brought against him, and has the power
of depriving him of his office. The Warden is not
an absolute sovereign ; the thirteen seniors are
associated with him in the government of the College,
and the Sub-Warden and five seniors are to inspect
his accounts once a year. At the periodical scrutinies,
when the conduct of all the members of the College
is to be examined, accusations can be brought
against him and duly investigated. This custom,
and others of Walter de Merton's regulations, were
clearly borrowed from the rules of monastic houses,
and a company of secular clerks seems to have had
difficulty in realising that they were bound by them,
for as early as 1284 the Archbishop of Canterbury,
who had become the Visitor of the College, had to
issue a series of orders for the observances of the
statutes. The Warden and Fellows of Merton had
permitted the study of medicine : they had interpreted too liberally the permission to study law ;

they had increased their own allowances and the salaries of their brewer and their cook ; the Fellows had resisted the authority of the Warden ; they had neglected the attendances at divine service enjoined by the Founder, and they had been lax about expulsions. The change which Walter de Merton had made in a scholar's life was so far-reaching that a secular would probably not have shared the astonishment of Archbishop Peckham (himself a friar) at the unwillingness of the Merton scholars to recognise the loss of their traditional freedom.

The system inaugurated by Walter de Merton was destined to have a great development. In the document of 1284, Peckham speaks of Merton as a " College," and its Founder was the founder of the Oxford College system. Although he repeated in his last statutes his permission to move his Society from Oxford, he regarded Oxford as its permanent home. Now that the civil war was over and England at peace, he had, he says, purchased a place of habitation and a house at Oxford, " where a University of students is flourishing." Not only had he provided a dwelling-place, he had also magnificently rebuilt a parish church to serve as a College-Chapel. The example he set was followed both at Oxford and at Cambridge, and the rule of Merton became the model on which College founders based elaborate codes of statutes. English founders generally followed Walter de Merton in making their societies self-governing communities, with an external Visitor as the ultimate court of appeal. There were in many colleges " poor boys " who were taught grammar, performed menial offices, and were not members, nor always eligible for election as members, of the Society ; but as a general rule the Fellows or Socii all had a share in the management of the affairs of the House. Routine business was frequently managed by the Head, the officers, and a limited number of the Senior Fellows, but the whole body of Fellows took part in the election of a new Head. A period of probation, varying from one year to three, was generally prescribed before an entrant was admitted a " full and perpetual " Fellow, and during this period of probation he had no right of voting. This restriction was sometimes dispensed with in the case of " Founder's kin," who became full Fellows at once, and the late Sir Edward Wingfield used to boast that in his Freshman term (1850) he had twice voted in opposition to the Warden of New College in a College meeting. As in a monastic house, this freedom was combined with a strict rule of obedience, and though the Head of a medieval College might be irritated by incidents of this kind, he possessed great dignity and high authority within his domain. As founders did more for their students, they expected a larger obedience from them, and attempted to secure it by minute regulations ; and the authority of the Head of the College increased with the number of rules which he was to enforce. The foundation of New College at Oxford in 1379 marks the completion of the collegiate ideal which had advanced so rapidly under the successive constitutions of Merton College a hundred years before. William of Wykeham, in providing for the needs of his scholars, availed himself of the experience of the past and created a new model for the future. The Fellows of New College were to be efficiently equipped at Winchester for the studies of the University, and, as we shall see, they were to receive in College special instruction in addition to the teaching of the University. Their magnificent home included, besides their living-rooms, a noble chapel and hall, a library, a garden, and a beautiful cloister for religious processions and for the burial of the dead. King Henry VI. built a still more magnificent house for his Cambridge scholars, and his example was followed by Henry VIII. The later College-founders, as we have said, expected obedience in proportion to their munificence, and the simpler statutes of earlier colleges were frequently revised and assimilated to those of later foundations. We reserve for a later section what we have to say about education, and deal here with habits and customs.

The Merton rule that conversation must be in Latin is generally found in College statutes. At Peterhouse, French might occasionally be spoken, should just and reasonable cause arise, but English very rarely. At New College, Latin was to be spoken even in the garden, though English might be used in addressing a layman. At Queen's College, Oxford, which was founded by a courtier, French was allowed as a regular alternative for Latin, and at Jesus College, Oxford, conversation might be in Greek, Latin, or Hebrew. In spite of the influence of the Renaissance, it seems unlikely that either Greek or Hebrew was much used as an alternative to Latin, but the Latin-speaking rule had become less rigid, and in sixteenth-century statutes more generous provision is made for dispensations from it. The Latin rule was not merely an educational method ; it was deliberately intended to be a check upon conversation. College founders accepted the apostolic maxim that the tongue worketh great evil, and they were convinced that a golden rule of silence was a protection against both ribaldry and quarrels. In the later statutes of Clare, the legislator recognises that not merely loss of time, but the creation of a disposition to be interested in trifles can be traced to " frequentes collocutiones," and he forbids any meetings in bedrooms (even meetings of Masters of Arts) for the purpose of feasting or of talking. If anyone wishes to receive a friend at dinner or supper, he must apply to the Master for leave, and such leave is to be very rarely given. Conversation in Hall was prohibited by the rule of silence and by the provision of a reader, which we have already found at Merton. The book read was almost invariably the Bible. William of Wykeham, who was followed in this, as in other respects, by later College founders, forbade his scholars to remain in Hall after dinner or supper, on the ground that they were likely to talk scandal and quarrel ; but on great Feast days, when a fire was allowed in the Hall, they might sit round and indulge in canticles and in listening to poems and chronicles and "mundi hujus mirabilia." The words of the statute (which reappear in those of later colleges) seem to imply that even on winter evenings a fire burned in the Hall only on Feast days, and the medieval student must have suffered severely from cold. There were, as a rule, no fire-places in private rooms until the sixteenth century, when we find references to them, *e.g.* in the statutes of Corpus Christi College, Oxford ; and the wooden shutters which took the place of windows shut out the scanty light of a winter day. When a Disputation (*cf.* p. 146) was held in Hall at night, a fire was lit, but we are not told how, when there was no Disputation or College meeting, the medieval

student spent the time between supper and the
" nightcap " which accompanied Compline. Dinner
was at ten in the morning and supper at six in the
evening. Dr Caius, in the middle of the sixteenth
century, ordered his students to be in bed by eight
o'clock in the evening, and " early to bed " must
have been the custom on winter nights in a medieval
College. " Early to rise " was the stern law, even
in the dark mornings, for the student's day began
at six o'clock, and he must often have listened to
lectures which commenced in the dark, although
dawn overtook the lecturer before he finished his
long exposition. In early times there was no
provision for breakfast, and, though the existence
of such a meal is distinctly contemplated in the
statutes of Queen's College, Oxford, there is no
hint of it in those of New College. Probably some
informal meal was usual everywhere, and was either
paid for privately or winked at by the authorities.
The absence of any general provision for breakfast
led to its being taken in private rooms and not in
Hall, and this is the humble origin of the College
breakfast party.

The number of occupants of a single room varied
in different colleges. Special provision was made
in later College statutes for the Head of the College ;
at New College he was given (for the first time) a
separate establishment and an allowance of plate

and kitchen utensils ; he was to dine in Hall only on some twenty great Feasts of the Church, and to sit at a separate table on these occasions. Henry VI. followed this precedent at King's, and elsewhere we find that the Head of a College is to have " principalem mansionem " with garden and stabling for the horses, without which it was not becoming that he should travel on College business. It was generally the duty of the Head to apportion the rooms among other members of the College, and to see that the juniors were under proper supervision. At Peterhouse, and in many other colleges, there were to be two in each chamber. When William of Wykeham built on a large scale, he ordered that there should be four occupants in the ground-floor rooms and three in the first-floor rooms. At King's, the numbers were three in ground-floor rooms and two in first-floor rooms. At Magdalen, the numbers were the same as at New College, but two of the beds in the upper rooms and one in the lower were to be " lectuli rotales, *Trookyll beddys* vulgariter appellati." Separate beds were usually provided, though sometimes boys under fourteen or fifteen years of age were denied this luxury. The bedrooms were also studies ; at Oxford there was no general sitting-room, except in monastic colleges, though Cambridge College statutes speak of a " parlura," corresponding to the modern parlour or combination room.

Each of the occupants of a room in New College was the proprietor of a small window, at which he worked, probably at some "study" or desk like the old Winchester "toys." The rooms had four windows and four "studiorum loca," and the general type of a College chamber, after the foundation of New College, was a room with one large window, and two, three, or four small windows for "studies."

A large proportion of the care of statute-makers was devoted to the prohibition of amusements. The statutes of Peterhouse forbade dogs or falcons, "for if one can have them in the House, all will want them, and so there will arise a constant howling" to disturb the studious. Dice and chess, being forbidden games to clerks, were also prohibited, and the scholars of Peterhouse were forbidden to frequent taverns, to engage in trade, to mix with actors, or to attend theatrical performances. These enactments are repeated in later College statutes, with such additions as the legislator's knowledge of human nature dictated and with occasional explanations of some interest in themselves. The keeping of dogs is often described as "taking the children's bread and giving it to dogs," and the Founder of Queen's College, Oxford, ordered that no animals were to be kept under the Fellows' rooms, since purity of air is essential for study. William of Wykeham expressly forbade chess,

which he classed with games leading to the loss
of money or estate, but King Henry VI., who made
large use of the statutes of New College, omitted the
mention of chess from his King's College statutes,
while he added to Wykeham's denunciation of
ferrets and hawks, an *index expurgatorius* of animals
which included monkeys, bears, wolves, and stags,
and he expressly forbade nets for hunting or fishing.
The principle on which modern Deans of colleges
have sometimes decided that "gramophones are
dogs" and therefore to be excluded from College,
can be traced in numerous regulations against
musical instruments, which disturb the peace essential to learning. That the medieval student felt
the temptations of "ragging" in much the same
way as his modern successors, appears from many
threats directed against those who throw stones and
other missiles to the danger of the buildings. Wykeham thought it necessary to forbid the throwing
of stones in Chapel, to the danger of the windows
and reredos, and for the safety of the reredos he
prohibited dancing or jumping in the Hall, which is
contiguous to the Chapel. Games in the Hall were
also forbidden for the comfort of the chaplains who
lived in the rooms underneath. King Henry VI.
forbade dancing or jumping, or other dangerous and
improper games in the Chapel, cloister, stalls, and
Hall of King's College.

Other disciplinary regulations common to all colleges deal with carrying arms, unpunctuality, talking during the reading in Hall or disturbing the Chapel services, bringing strangers into College, sleeping out of College, absence without leave, negligence and idleness, scurrilous or offensive language, spilling water in upper rooms to the detriment of the inhabitants of the lower rooms, and failure to attend the regular " scrutinies " or the stated general meetings for College business. At these scrutinies, any serious charges against members of the Society were considered, and it is in keeping with some of the judicial ideas of the time that some statutes forbid the accused person to have a copy of the indictment against him. For contumacy, for grave moral offences, for crimes of violence, and for heresy, the penalty was expulsion. Less serious offences were punished by subtraction of " commons," *i.e.* deprivation of allowances for a day or a week (or longer), or by pecuniary fines. When College founders provided clothes as well as board and lodging for their scholars, the forfeiture of a robe took its place among the penalties with which offenders were threatened. The " poor boys " who sang in Chapel and waited on the Fellows were whipped like boys elsewhere, who were being taught grammar, but the birch was unknown as a punishment for undergraduates till late in the

E

middle ages. The introduction of corporal punishment into college life in England may be traced by a comparison of William of Wykeham's statutes with those of Henry VI. The King's College statute " De correctionibus faciendis circa delicta leviora " is largely a transcript of a New College statute, with the same title, and both contemplate subtraction of commons as the regular penalty. But the King's College statute contains an additional clause, to the effect that scholars and younger Fellows may be punished with stripes. In the statutes of Magdalen, dated some seventeen years later, William of Waynflete returned to the New College form of the statute, but he provided that his demys (i.e. scholars who received half the commons of a Fellow) should be subject to the penalty of whipping in the Grammar School. The statutes of Christ's College prescribe a fine of a farthing for unpunctuality on the part of the scholars studying in the Faculty of Arts, and heavier fines for absence, and it is added that if the offender be not an adult, a whipping is to be substituted for the pecuniary penalty. At Brasenose, where the Fellows were all of the standing of at least a Bachelor of Arts, the undergraduate scholars were subjected to an unusually strict discipline, and offenders were to be punished either by fines or by the rod, the Principal deciding the appropriate punishment in each case. For unpunctuality, for negligence and idleness, for playing, laughing, talking, making a noise or speaking English in a lecture-room, for insulting fellow-students, or for disobedience to his pastors and masters, the Brasenose undergraduate was to be promptly flogged. Among the crimes for which the birch is ordered we find " making odious comparisons," a phrase which throws some light on the conversational subjects of sixteenth-century undergraduates. The kind of comparison is indicated in the statute ; remarks about the country, the family, the manners, the studies, and the ability, or the person, of a fellow-student must be avoided. Similarly, at Jesus College, Cambridge, it is forbidden to compare country to country, race to race, or science to science, and William of Wykeham and other founders had to make similar injunctions. The medieval student was distinctly quarrelsome, and such records as the famous Merton " scrutiny " of 1339, and investigations by College Visitors, show that the seniors set the undergraduates a bad example. The statutes of Corpus Christi College, Oxford, provide for two new penalties. An offending undergraduate might be sentenced to feed by himself, at a small table in the middle of the Hall, and in aggravated cases to the monastic penalty of bread and water. An alternative penalty was detention in the library at the most inconvenient

time ("per horam vel horas cum minime vellet"),
and the performance of an imposition to be shown
up in due course. The rough and ready penalty
of the birch is, however, frequently mentioned in
the statutes of Corpus and of other sixteenth-century
Colleges. Cardinal Wolsey thought it proper that
an undergraduate should be whipped until he had
completed his twentieth year. At Trinity, Cambridge (where offenders were sociably flogged before
the assembled College on Friday evenings) the age
was eighteen. Dr Caius restricted the rod to
scholars who were not adult. "We call those
adults," he says, "who have completed their
eighteenth year. For before that age, both in
ancient times and in our own memory, youth was
not accustomed to wear *braccas*, being content with
tibialia reaching to the knees." The stern dis-
ciplinarian might find an excuse for prolonging the
whipping age in the Founder's wish that, "years
alone should not make an adult, but along with
years, gravity of deportment and good character."
As late as the foundation of Pembroke College at
Oxford (1624) whipping is the penalty contemplated for undergraduates under eighteen. But
when we come to the statutes which were drawn
up in 1698 with a view to the foundation of Wor-
cester College, not only is there no mention of the
birch, but even pecuniary penalties are deprecated

for minor offences, for which impositions and gating are suggested.

Minor penalties were enforced by the Head of a college, the Vice-Head, the Deans, and, in sixteenth-century colleges, by the tutors. By later college statutes, these officers received for their personal use a portion of the fines they inflicted, and appeals were sometimes permitted from an officer to the Head, and even to the Chancellor or Vice-Chancellor of the University. The oath taken by scholars frequently bound them to reveal to the authorities, any breach of the statutes, and there are indications that members of the College were encouraged to report each other's misdeeds. Thus the Master of Christ's is to fine anyone whom he hears speaking one complete sentence in English, or anyone whom he may know to have been guilty of this offence, except in sleeping-rooms or at times when permission had been given.

Oxford and Cambridge Colleges were, as we have seen, endowed homes for the education of secular clerks. All of them, on entrance, had to have the tonsure, and provision was often made for the cutting of their hair and beard. At Christ's College, there was a regular College barber " qui . . . caput et barbam radet ac tondebit hebdomadis singulis." They wore ordinary clerical dress, and undue expenditure on clothes and ornaments was strictly prohibited, *e.g.* the Fellows of Peterhouse were forbidden to wear rings on their fingers " ad inanem gloriam et jactantiam." The early founders did not insist upon Holy Orders for the Heads or Fellows of their colleges, though many of them would naturally proceed to the priesthood, but in later college statutes all the Fellows were ultimately to proceed, at stated times, to Holy Orders and to the priesthood, though dispensations for delay might be granted, and students of Medicine were sometimes excused from the priesthood. When they became priests they were, like other priests, to celebrate mass regularly in the Chapel, but were not to receive payment for celebrations outside the College. As mere tonsured undergraduates, they were not, at first, subject to regulations for daily attendance at divine service ; but later founders were stricter in this, as in other matters. Bishop Bateman, who, in the middle of the fourteenth century, legislated for the infant Gonville College, ordered that every Fellow should hear one mass daily and say certain prayers, and in his own foundation of Trinity Hall, he repeated the injunction. The prescribed prayers included petitions for the Founder, or for the repose of his soul ; every Fellow of Trinity Hall was to say, immediately upon rising in the morning and before going to bed at night, the prayer " Rege quaesumus Domine," during the Bishop's lifetime, and after

his death, " Deus qui inter Apostolicos Sacerdotes,"
and to say the psalm " De profundis clamavi " and
a " Kurie eleeson " for the repose of the soul of the
Founder's father and mother, his predecessors in
the see of Norwich, and after his death for his own
soul. The ten priests who served the Chapel at
New College, said masses for the Founder and his
benefactors, but every Fellow was to attend mass
every day and to say prayers in his own room,
morning and evening, including " Rege, quaesumus,
Domine, Willielmum Pontificem Fundatorem
nostrum " or, after his death, " Deus qui inter
Apostolicos sacredotes famulum tuum Fundatorem
nostrum pontificali dignitate " ; and every day,
both after High Mass in Chapel, and after dinner
and supper in Hall, the psalm " De profundis " was
said. Penalties were prescribed for negligence, and
as time went on, a whipping was inflicted for absence
from Chapel, *e.g.* at Christ's College, and at Balliol,
for which new statutes were drawn up in 1507.

Residence in College was continuous throughout
the year, even during the University vacation,
which lasted from early in July to the beginning of
October. Leave of absence might be granted at
any time in the year, on reasonable grounds, but was
to be given generally in vacations. General rules
were laid down for behaviour in keeping with the
clerical profession during absence, and students on

leave were forbidden to frequent taverns or otherwise transgress the rules which were binding upon them in the University. Occasionally we find some relaxation in these strict regulations, as when the Founder of Corpus Christi at Oxford allows " moderate hunting or hawking " when one of his scholars is on holiday away from Oxford. The same indulgent Founder, after the usual prohibition of games in College, allows a game of ball in the garden for the sake of healthy exercise. (" Non prohibemus tamen lusum pilae ad murum, tabulata, aut tegulas, in horto, causa solum modo exercendi corporis et sanitatis.") Associations with home life were maintained by vacation visits, but the influx of " people " to the University was, of course, unknown. The ancient statutes of Peterhouse permit a woman (even if she be not a relation) to talk with a Fellow in the Hall, preferably in the presence of another Fellow, or at least, a servant ; but the legislator had grave fears of the results of such " confabulationes," and the precedent he set was not followed. A Fellow or scholar is frequently permitted by College statutes to entertain his father, brother, nephew, or a friend, obtaining first the consent of the Head of the College, and paying privately for the entertainment, but no such guest might sleep in College, and the permission is carefully restricted to the male sex. Women were, as a rule, not allowed within a College gate ; if it was impossible to find a man to wash clothes, a laundress might be employed, but she must be old and of unprepossessing appearance. A scholar or Fellow of a college had not, however, committed himself irrevocably to a celibate life, for marriage is included among the " causas rationabiles et honestas " which vacated a fellowship. It was possible, though probably infrequent, for a Fellow who had not proceeded to Holy Orders to leave the College " uxore ducta," giving up his emolument, his clerical dress, and the tonsure. Even if a Fellow enjoyed the Founder's provision for the long period of his course in Arts and Theology, and proceeded in due time to Holy Orders, it was not contemplated that he should remain a Fellow till his death.

> " . . . he had geten him yet no benefyce,
> Ne was so worldly for to have offyce,"

says Chaucer, indicating the natural end of a scholar's career. He might betake himself to some " obsequium," and rise high in the service of the king, or of some great baron or bishop, and become, like one of Wykeham's first New College scholars, Henry Chichele, an archbishop and a College founder himself. Should no such great career open up for him, he can, at the least, succeed to one of the livings which the founders of English colleges purchased for this purpose. His " obsequium "

would naturally lead to his ceasing to reside, and
so vacate his fellowship, and his acceptance of a
benefice over a certain value brought about the
same result. Some such event was expected to
happen to every Fellow ; unless he happened to be
elected to the Headship, it was not intended that
he should grow old in the College, and at Queen's
College, Oxford, the arbitrary or unreasonable refusal
of a benefice vacated a Fellowship. The object of
the College Founder was, that there should never
be wanting a succession of men qualified to serve
God in Church and State, and to Chaucer's unworldly
clerk, if he was a member of a College, there would
come, in due course, the country living and good-
bye to the University. But statutes were not always
strictly observed and the idle life-Fellow, who survived to be the scandal of early Victorian days, was
not unknown in the end of the Middle Ages.

One of the causes of vacating a fellowship throws
some light upon the class of men who became
members of Oxford and Cambridge Colleges. The
opening sentences of founders' statutes usually
contain some such phrase as " collegium pauperum
et indigentium scholarium " ; but later sections of
the statutes contemplate the possibility of their
succeeding to property—" patrimonium, haeredi-
tatem, feudumve saeculare, vel pensionem annuam "
—and if such property exceeded the annual value of

a hundred shillings, a Fellowship was *ipso facto* vacated. The " pauperes et indigentes " expressions must not be construed too literally ; the Founder was establishing a claim to the merits of him that considereth the poor, and the language he used was part of the ordinary formulas of the time, and ought not to be interpreted more strictly than the ordinary phrases of legal and Diplomatic documents or than the conventional terms of courtesy, which begin and conclude a modern letter. That an English College Founder wished to give help where help was required, is undeniable, but help was required by others than the poorest. The advancement of the study of theology was near the heart of every medieval founder, and the study of theology demanded the surrender of the best years of a man's life, and the extension of the period of education long after he might be expected to be earning his own living. A curriculum in the University which covered at least sixteen years, and might be followed by nothing more remunerative than the cure of Chaucer's poor priest, required some substantial inducement if it was to attract the best men. Canon Law, Civil Law and Medicine, if they offered more opportunity of attaining a competency, required also a very long period of apprenticeship in the University. There were many youths in the Middle Ages (as there are to-day) neither " pauperes "

nor "indigentes" in the strict sense of the word,
but too poor to be able to afford sixteen years of
study in the University. The length of the medieval
curriculum produced some of the necessities which
colleges were established to meet.

That the founders were not thinking of the
poorest classes of the community, is evident from
many provisions of their statutes. They frequently
provided only board and lodging, and left their
beneficiaries to find elsewhere the other necessities
of life ; they appointed penalties (such as the subtraction of commons for a month) which would have
meant starvation to the penniless ; they contemplated entertainments and journeys, and in the case
of a New College Doctor, even the maintenance of a
private servant, at the personal expense of their
scholars and Fellows ; they prohibited the expenditure of money on extravagant dress and
amusements. William of Wykeham made allowances for the expense of proceeding to degrees
in the University when one of his Fellows had
no private means and no friends to assist him
("propter paupertatem, inopiam, et penuriam,
carentiamque amicorum ") ; but the sum to be
thus administered was strictly limited and the
recipient had to prove his poverty, and to swear to
the truth of his statement. The very frequent
insistence upon provisions for a Founder's kin,

suggests that the society, to which he wished a large number of his relations to belong, was of higher social standing than an almshouse ; and the liberal allowances for the food of the Fellows, as contrasted with the sums allotted to servants and choristers, show that life in College was intended to be easy, and comfortable. The fact that menial work was to be done by servants and that Fellows were to be waited on at table by the " poor boys " is a further indication of the dignity of the Society. At New College, it was the special duty of one servant to carry to the schools, the books of the Fellows and scholars. The possession of considerable means by a medieval Fellow, is illustrated by two wills, printed in " Munimenta Academica." Henry Scayfe, Fellow of Queen's College, left in 1449, seven pounds to his father, smaller sums to a large number of friends, including sixpence to every scholar of the College, and also disposed by will of sheep, cattle and horses. In 1457, John Seggefyld, Fellow of Lincoln College, bequeathed to his brother tenements in Kingston by Hull, which had been left him by his father, twelve pence to each of his colleagues, and thirteen shillings and four pence to his executor. Whether the possessions of these men ought to have led to the resignation of their Fellowships, is a question which may have interested their colleagues at the time ; to us the facts are important, as illustrating the private means of members of a society of "poor and indigent" scholars, and as indicating the class from which such scholars were drawn.

College regulations in other countries add considerably to our knowledge of medieval student-life. In Paris, where the system had its humble beginning in the hire of a room for eighteen poor scholars, by a benevolent Englishman returning from a pilgrimage to Palestine in 1180, the college ideal progressed slowly and never reached its highest development. Even when most of the students of Paris came to live in colleges, the college was not the real unit of university life, nor was a Parisian college a self-governing community like Merton or Peterhouse. The division of the University of Paris into Nations affected its social life, and the Faculties were separated at Paris in a manner unknown in England. A college at Paris was organised in accordance with Faculty divisions, an arrangement so little in harmony with the ideas of English founders, that William of Wykeham provided that Canonists and Civilists, should be mixed in chambers with students of other Faculties "ad nutriendam et conservandam majorem dilectionem, amicitiam et charitatem inter eosdem." As colleges at Paris were frequently confined to natives of a particular district, they tended to become sub-divisions of the Nations. The disadvantages of restricting membership of a college to a diocese or locality, were seen and avoided by the founder of the College of Sorbonne, in the middle of the thirteenth century, and the founder of the sixteenth century College of Mans protested against the custom, by instructing his executors to open his foundation to men, from every nation and province, insisting that association with companions of different languages and customs, would make the scholars " civiliores, eloquentiores, et doctiores," and that the friendships thus formed would enable them to render better service to the State. The tenure of his *bursa* or emolument, by a member of a Paris college, was so precarious that he could not count upon proceeding to a higher Faculty in his own college, and the existence of an outside body of governors and of Patrons or Visitors, who had the power of filling up vacancies further checked the growth of corporate feeling and college patriotism. The large powers entrusted to an external authority made the position of the Head of a college at Paris, much less important than at Oxford or Cambridge.

The differences between English and Parisian colleges may best be realised by a reference to the statutes of some early Paris founders. About 1268, Guillaume de Saone, Treasurer of Rouen, founded at Paris the " Treasurer's College " for natives of his

own diocese. It was founded for poor clerks,
twelve of whom were to be scholars in Theology,
and twelve in Arts. They were to be selected by
the archdeacons of the Cathedral of Rouen, who
then resided at Grand-Caux and Petit-Caux, from
natives of these places, or, failing them, from the
Diocese of Rouen. The scholars were to have
rooms and a weekly allowance, not for the whole
year, but for forty-five weeks from the feast of St
Dionysius ; no provision was made for the seven
weeks of the vacation, except for two theologians,
who were to take charge of the house at Paris.
The revenues were collected and distributed by the
Prior of the Hospital of St Mary Magdalen at Rouen,
and the Archbishop of Rouen was Rector and Patron.
The students in Arts never formed part of the
foundation, for the Treasurer almost immediately
restricted his community to Theologians, and their
tenure of the endowment was strictly limited to
two years after obtaining their licence. " For we
do not wish to grant them anything more, because
our intention is only to induce them to proceed to the
degree of master in theology." They were furnished
with books, which they were forbidden to lend,
and they were placed under the immediate super-
intendence of the senior Bursar or Foundationer,
whose duty it was to call them together once a week,
and inquire into their conduct and their progress in

their studies. Some general rules were laid down by the Founder, and offenders against them were to be expelled at these meetings. They were permitted to receive a peaceful commoner, who paid for his chamber and was a student of Theology. The interest of the Treasurer of Rouen in Theology is characteristic, and the great College of the Sorbonne, founded about the same time, was also restricted to theologians. The College of Navarre, founded in 1304, provided for twenty students of grammar, twenty in logic and philosophy (Arts) and twenty in Theology, each Faculty forming a sub-college, with a separate hall. A doctor in grammar was to superintend both the studies and the morals of the grammarians and to receive double their weekly allowance of four shillings, and similarly, a master of Arts was to supervise the Artists and receive double their weekly allowance of six shillings. The " Dean and University of the masters of the scholars of the theological Faculty at Paris " were to choose a secular clerk to be Rector of the College, and to govern it in conjunction with the body that appointed him. The masters of the Faculty of Theology, or their representatives, were to visit the College annually, to inquire into the financial and domestic arrangements, and into the behaviour of the Rector, masters, and scholars, and to punish as they deemed necessary. Membership of the

F

College was restricted to the kingdom of France. Similarly, the College du Plessis, founded in 1322, by Geoffrey du Plessis, Notary Apostolic, and Secretary of Philip the Long, was restricted to Frenchmen, with preference to certain northern dioceses. Its forty scholars were in separate societies, with a Grand Master who had to be a master or, at least, a bachelor in Theology. The affairs of the College, as far as concerned the election, discipline and the deprivation of its members, were to be administered by two bishops and an abbot, in conjunction with the Master and with the Chancellor of the Cathedral of Paris, or, in the absence of the great dignitaries, by the Master and the Chancellor. But the financial administration was entrusted to a provisor or procurator, who undertook the collection and distribution of the revenues.

The details of college statutes at Paris, bear a general resemblance to the regulations of Oxford and Cambridge founders, and discipline became more stringent as time went on. Attendance at Chapel (the only meeting-place of students in different Faculties in the same College) came to be strictly required. Punctuality at meals was frequently insisted upon, under pain of receiving nothing but bread. Silence was enjoined at meal times and the Bible was read. Latin was, from the first, the only lawful medium of conversation. All the members of a college, had to be within the gates when the curfew bell rang. Bearing arms or wearing unusual clothes was forbidden, and singing, shouting and games were denounced as interfering with the studies of others, although the Parisian legislators were more sympathetic with regard to games, than their English contemporaries. Even the Founder of the Cistercian College of St Bernard, contemplated that permission might be obtained for games, though not before dinner or after the bell rang for vespers. A sixteenth-century code of statutes for the College of Tours, while recording the complaints of the neighbours about the noise made by the scholars playing ball (" de insolentiis, exclamationibus et ludis palmariis dictorum scolarium, qui ludunt . . . pilis durissimis ") permitted the game under less noisy conditions (" pilis seu scophis mollibus et manu, ac cum silentio et absque clamoribus tumultuosis "). The use of dice was, as a rule, absolutely prohibited, but the statutes of the College of Cornouaille permitted it under certain conditions. It might be played to amuse a sick fellow on feast days, or without the plea of sickness, on the vigils of Christmas, and of three Holy Days. But the stakes must be small and paid in kind, not in money (" pro aliquo comestibili vel potabili ").

Penalties for minor offences were much the same as in England—forfeiture of commons for varying

periods, pecuniary fines, and in the sixteenth
century, whipping. In the College of Le Mans,
bursars who were not graduates were to be whipped
for a first offence in a school, and for a second
offence in the Hall (" prout mos est in universit-
ate Parisiensi "). The obligation of reporting each
other's faults, of which there are indications in
English statutes, was almost universal at Paris, where
all were bound to reveal offences " sub secreto "
to the authorities. The penalty of " sconcing,"
still inflicted at Oxford, for offences against undergraduate etiquette, finds a place in the Parisian
statutes among serious punishments. We find it
in the Statutes of Cornouaille for minor offences ;
if a man carries wine out of the College illicitly, he
is to pay for double the quantity, to be drunk by
the members who were present at the time ; if
anyone walks through the confines or chambers in
pattens (" cum calepodiis, id est cum patinis ") he is
to be mulcted in a pint of wine. If a stranger is
introduced without leave (" ad mensam communitatis
ad comedendum vel videndum secretum mensae "),
the penalty is a quart of good wine for the fellows
present in Hall. For unseemly noise, especially at
meals, and at time of prayers, the ordinary penalty
is a quart of ordinary wine (" vini mediocris "). For
speaking in the vernacular, there is a fine of " the
price of a pint of wine," but, as the usual direction

about drinking it, is omitted, this was probably not
a sconce ; at the Cistercian College, the penalty for
this offence was a sconce. So far, the offences for
which a sconce is prescribed, might in most cases,
be paralleled in more recent times in an English
college, but the statutes of Cornouaille also make
sconcing the penalty for striking a servant, unless
the injury was severe, in which case, more serious
punishments were imposed. The whole sentence
is an illustration of the lack of control over outbursts
of bad temper, which is characteristic of medieval
life. All the scholars are to be careful not to strike
the servants in anger or with ill-will, or to injure them :
he who inflicts a slight injury is to be fined a quart
of wine ; if the injury be more severe, the master
is to deprive him of his burse for one day or more,
at his own discretion and that of a majority of the
scholars : if there is a large effusion of blood or a
serious injury, the provisor (the Bishop of Paris or
his Vicar General) is to be informed, and to deprive
the offender of his burse, or even punish him otherwise. At the Sorbonne, an assault on a servant was
to be followed by the drinking of a quart of specially good wine by the Fellows, at the culprit's
expense ; for talking too loud in Hall, the sconce
was two quarts (presumably of ordinary wine).
Dr Rashdall quotes from the MS. Register of the
Sorbonne, actual instances of the infliction of

sconces : " A Doctor of Divinity is sconced a quart
of wine for picking a pear off a tree in the College
garden, or again, for forgetting to shut the Chapel
door, or for taking his meals in the kitchen. Clerks
are sconced a pint for ' very inordinately ' knock-
ing ' at the door during dinner . . .' for ' con-
fabulating ' in the court late at night, and refusing
to go to their chambers when ordered. . . . The
head cook is sconced for ' badly preparing the
meat for supper,' or for not putting salt in the
soup." Among the examples given by Dr Rashdall
from this source are a sconce of two shillings for
drunkenness and a sconce in wine inflicted upon the
head cook for being found " cum una meretrice."
An offence so serious in a bursar, is by many college
statutes to be followed by expulsion, and Dr Rashdall
quotes an instance of this penalty : but Parisian
College Founders, were less severe in dealing with
moral offences than English Founders. At the
monastic College of Marmoutier, it was only on the
second offence that bringing into College (" mulierem
suspectam et inhonestam ") led to expulsion, and at
the College of Cornouaille, the penalty for a first
offence was loss of commons or bursa for fifteen
days, and for a second offence a month's deprivation ;
but even at Cornouaille actual incontinence was to
be punished by expulsion.

A late code of statutes of the fourteenth-century

College of Dainville, give us a picture of a student's day. The hour of rising was five o'clock, except on Sundays and Feast days when an hour's grace was allowed. Chapel service began at 5.30, prayers, meditation, and a New Testament lesson being followed by the mass of the College at six. All students resident in the College had to be present. The reception of commoners, an early instance of which we noted in the College of the Treasurer, had developed to such an extent, that all Colleges had, in addition to their bursars or foundations, a large number of " foranei scholares," who paid their own expenses but were subject to College discipline, and received a large part of their education in College. After mass, the day's work began ; attendance at the Schools and the performance of exercises for their master in College. Dinner was about twelve o'clock, when either a bursar or an external student read, " first Holy Scripture, then a book appointed by the master, then a passage from a martyrology." After dinner, an hour was allowed for recreation—walking within the precincts of the College, or conversation—and then everyone went to his own chamber. Supper was at seven, with reading as at dinner, and the interval until 8.30 was again free for " deambulatio vel collocutio." At 8.30 the gates of the College were closed, and evening Chapel began. Rules against remaining in Hall after supper occur in Parisian as well as in English statutes, and we find prohibitions against carrying off wood to private rooms. The general arrangement of Parisian college chambers, probably resembled those of Oxford, or Cambridge, and we find references to " studies." The statutes of the monastic college of Clugny order that " because the mind is rendered prudent by sitting down and keeping quiet, the said students at the proper and wonted hours for study shall be, and sit, alone in their cells and at their studies." Parisian statutes are stricter than English statutes in insisting upon frequent inspections of students' chambers, and a sixteenth-century code for a Parisian college orders the officials to see their pupils every night before bed time, and to make sure, before they themselves retire for the night, that the students are asleep and not wandering about the quadrangles.

Strict supervision is found in colleges in other French universities, even in those which belong to the student type. It was, of course, especially strict in monastic colleges, which carried their own customs to the University ; in the College of Notre Dame de Pitié, at Avignon, the master of the novices lived in a room adjoining their dormitory, and had a window, through which he might watch their proceedings. Supervision was sometimes connected with precautions against fire, e.g. at the College of

Saint Ruf, at Montpellier, an officer was appointed every week to go round all chambers and rooms at night, and to warn anyone who had a candle or a fire in a dangerous position, near his bed or his study. He was to carry a pail of water with him to be ready for emergencies. A somewhat similar precaution was taken in the Collegium Maius at Leipsic, where water was kept in pails beside the dormitories, and leather pails, some centuries old, are still to be seen at Oxford. As a rule, the dormitories seem to have contained a separate bed for each occupant, but in the College of St Nicholas de Pelegry at Cahors, students in arts (who entered about the age of fourteen) were to sleep two in a bed. Insistence on the use of Latin is almost universal ; the scholars of the College de Foix at Toulouse are warned that only ploughmen, swineherds and other rustics, use their mother tongues. Silence and the reading of the Bible at meals was usual, and students are sometimes told to make their needs known, if possible, by signs. Fines for lateness at meals are common, and there are injunctions against rushing into Hall with violence and greed : no one is to go near the kitchen to seize any food, and those who enter Hall first, are to wait till the rest arrive, and all are to sit down in the proper order. Prohibitions against dogs are infrequent in the French statutes ; at the College des Douze Medecins at

Montpellier, one watchdog was allowed to live in
College. Women were often forbidden to enter a
college, " quia mulier caput est peccati, arma dyaboli,
expulsio paradysi, et corruptio legis antiquae."
The College of Saint Ruf at Montpellier, in the
statutes of which this formula occurs, did, however,
allow women to stand in the Chapel at mass, provided that they did not enter the choir. The
monastic institution of Our Lady of Pity at Avignon,
went so far as to have a matron for the young boys,
an old woman, entitled " Mater Novitiorum Col-
legiatorum." At the College of Breuil at Angers,
a woman might visit the College by day if the
Principal was satisfied that no scandal could arise.
Penalties for going about the town in masked
bands and singing or dancing, occur in many
statutes, but processions in honour of saints and
choruses to celebrate the taking of degrees, are
sometimes permitted. Blasphemy and bad language
greatly troubled the French statute-makers, and
there are many provisions against blaspheming the
Blessed Virgin. At the College of Breuil at Angers,
a fine of twopence, was imposed for speaking or
singing " verba inhonesta tam alte," especially in
public places of the College ; in Germany, the Collegium Minus at Leipsic provides also against
writing " impudentia dicta " on the walls of the
College. The usual penalties for minor offences

are fines and subtraction of commons : references to flogging are rare, though it is found in both French and German colleges. More serious crimes were visited with suspension and expulsion. At the College of Pelegry, at Cahors, to enter the college by a window or otherwise after the great gate was closed, involved rustication for two months for the first offence, six months for the second offence, and expulsion for a third. At the College de Verdale, at Toulouse, expulsion was the penalty for a list of crimes which includes theft, entering the college by stealth, breaking into the cellar, bringing in a meretrix, witch-craft, alchemy, invoking demons or sacrificing to them, forgery, and contracting " carnale vel spirituale matrimonium."

We may close our survey of the Medieval College, with a glimpse of a French college in the fourteenth century. We have the record of a visitation of the Benedictine foundation of St Benedict, at Mont-pellier, partly a monastery and partly a college. The Prior is strictly questioned about the conduct of the students. He gives a good character to most of them : but the little flock contained some black sheep. Peter is somewhat light-headed (" aliquan-tulum est levis capitis ") but not incorrigible ; he has been guilty of employing " verba injuriosa et pro-vocativa," but the Prior has corrected him, and he has taken the correction patiently. Bertrand's

life is " aliquantulum dissoluta," and he has made
a conspiracy to beat (and, as some think, to kill)
Dominus Savaricus, who had beaten him along
with the rest, when he did not know his lessons.
(Bertrand says he is eighteen and looks like twenty-
one, but this is a monastic college and the beating
is monastic discipline.)   The Prior further reports
that Bertrand is quarrelsome ; he has had to make
him change his bed and his chamber, because the
others could not stand him ; he is idle and often
says openly, that he would rather be a " claus-
tralis " than a student.   Breso is simple and easily
led, and was one of Bertrand's conspirators.   William
is " pessimae conversationis " and incorrigible,
scandalous in word and deed, idle and given to
wandering about the town.   Correction is vain in
his case.   After the Prior has reported, the students
are examined *viva voce* upon the portions of the
decretals, which they are studying, and the results
of the examination bear out generally the Prior's
views.   Bertrand, Breso and William, are found to
know nothing, and to have wasted their time.   The
others acquit themselves well, and the examiners
are merciful to a boy who is nervous in *viva voce*,
but of whose studies Dominus Savaricus, who has
recovered from the attack made upon him, gives a
good account.   Monks, and especially novices, were
human, and the experience of St Benedict's at

Montpellier was probably similar to that of secular colleges in France and elsewhere. Even in democratic Bologna, it was found necessary in the Spanish College (from the MS. statutes of which, Dr Rashdall quotes) to establish a discipline which included a penalty of five days in the stocks and a meal of bread and water, eaten sitting on the floor of the Hall, for an assault upon a brother student ; if blood was shed, the penalty was double. The statutes of the Spanish College were severe for the fourteenth century, and they penalise absence from lecture, unpunctuality, nocturnal wanderings and so forth, as strictly as any English founder.

CHAPTER V

THE growing tradition of strict college discipline ultimately led to disciplinary statutes in the universities. From very early times, universities had, of course, made regulations about the curriculum, and the border-line between a scholar's studies and his manners and morals, could not be absolutely fixed. At Paris, indeed, it is not until the fifteenth century that we find any detailed code of disciplinary statutes ; but fourteenth-century regulations about dress were partly aimed at checking misdeeds of students disguised as laymen, and in 1391 the English Nation prohibited an undue number of " potationes et convivia," in celebration of the " jocund advent " of a freshman or on other occasions. It was not till the middle of the fifteenth century that the University of Paris, awoke to the realisation of its own shortcomings in manners and morals ; Cardinal William de Estoutville was commissioned by Nicholas V. to reform it, and internal reform, the necessity of which had been recognised for some years, began about the same time with an edict of the Faculty of Arts ordering

a general improvement, and especially forbidding
the celebration of feasts "cum mimis seu instrumentis altis." Estoutville's ordinances are largely
concerned with the curriculum, he was at least as
anxious to reform the masters as the pupils, and his
exhortations are frequently in general or scriptural
terms. The points of undergraduate discipline on
which he lays stress are feasting, dressing impro-
perly or wearing the clothes of laymen, quarrelling,
and games and dances "dissolutas et inhonestas."
Four masters or doctors are to inspect annually the
colleges and pedagogies, in which the students live,
and are to see that proper discipline is maintained.
From time to time, similar regulations were made
by the Faculty of Arts, *e.g.* in 1469, it is ordered
that no student is to wear the habit of a fool, except
for a farce or a morality (amusements permitted at
this period). Any one carrying arms or wearing
fools' dress is to be beaten in public and in his own
hall. These last regulations are doubtless connected
with town and gown riots, for which the Feast of
Fools afforded a tempting opportunity.

The absence of disciplinary regulations in the
records of the University of Paris, is largely to be
explained by the fact that criminal charges against
Parisian scholars were tried in the Bishop's Court,
and civil actions in the Court of the Provost of
Paris. At Oxford, where the whole jurisdiction

belonged to the Chancellor of the University, disciplinary statutes are much more numerous. We find, from the middle of the thirteenth century onwards, a series of edicts against scholars who break the peace or carry arms, who enter citizens' houses to commit violence, who practise the art of sword and buckler, or who are guilty of gross immorality. A statute of 1250 forbids scholars to celebrate their national feast days disguised with masks or garlands, and one of 1313 restricts the carrying of arms to students who are entering on, or returning from, long journeys. Offenders who refuse to go to prison, or who escape from it, are to be expelled. As early as the middle of the thirteenth century, it was the duty of the proctors and of the principals of halls, to investigate into, and to report the misdeeds of scholars who broke the rules of the University or lived evil lives. A list of fines drawn up in 1432 (a period when in the opinion of the University a pecuniary penalty was more dreaded than anything else) prescribes fines of twelve pence for threatening violence, two shillings for wearing arms, four shillings for a violent shove with the shoulders or a blow with the fist, six shillings and eight pence for a blow with a stone or stick, ten shillings for a blow with a sword, a knife, a dagger or any similar " bellicose weapon," twenty shillings for carrying bows and arrows with evil intent, thirty shillings for collecting an assembly to break the peace, hinder the execution of justice, or make an attack upon anyone, and forty shillings for resisting the execution of justice or wandering about by night. In every case damages have also to be paid to any injured person. The device of overaweing a court (familiar in Scottish history) is prohibited by a regulation that no one shall appear before the Chancellor with more than two companions.

The records of the Chancellor's Court furnish us with instances of the enforcement of these regulations. In 1434, a scholar is found wearing a dagger and is sentenced to be " inbocardatus,"[1] *i.e.* imprisoned in the Tower of the North Gate of the city, and another offender, in 1442, suffers a day's imprisonment, pays his fine of two shillings, and forfeits his arms. In the same year, John Hordene, a scholar of Peckwater Inn, is fined six shillings and eightpence for breaking the head of Thomas Walker, manciple of Pauline Hall, and Thomas Walker is fined the like sum for drawing his sword on Hordene and for gambling. In 1433, two scholars, guilty of attacking Master Thomas Rygby in Bagley Wood and stealing twelve shillings and sevenpence from him, fail to appear, and are expelled from the University, their goods (estimated to be worth about

[1] The prison was called " Bocardo " because, like the mood known as " Bocardo " in the syllogism, it was difficult to get out of.

G

thirteen shillings) being confiscated. In 1457, four scholars are caught entering with weapons into a warren or park to hunt deer and rabbits; they are released on taking an oath that, while they are students of the University, they will not trespass again in closed parks or warrens. In 1452, a scholar of Haburdaysh Hall is imprisoned for using threatening language to a tailor, and is fined twelvepence and imprisoned; the tailor insults the prisoner and is fined six shillings and eightpence. We have quoted instances of undergraduate offences, but the evil-doers are by no means invariably young students, *e.g.* in 1457 the Vicar of St Giles has to take an oath to keep the peace, his club is forfeited, and he is fined two shillings; and in the same year the Master of St John's Hospital, who has been convicted of divers enormous offences, is expelled the University for breaking prison.

The increased stringency of disciplinary regulations at Oxford in the end of the medieval period is best illustrated by the statutes which, in the fifteenth century, the University enforced upon members of the unendowed Halls. Students who were not members of a College lived, for the most part, in one of the numerous Halls which, up to the Reformation, were so important a feature of the University. A code of these statutes, printed for the first time by Dr Rashdall, shows that the liberty of the earlier medieval undergraduate had largely disappeared, and that the life of a resident in a Hall, in the end of the fifteenth century, was almost as much governed by statute and regulation as if he were the partaker of a founder's bounty. He must hear mass and say matins and vespers every day, under pain of a fine of a penny, and attend certain services on feast days. His·table manners are no longer regulated by the customs and etiquette of his fellows, but by the rules of the University. His lapses from good morals are no longer to be visited with penalties imposed by his own society ; if he gambles or practises with sword and buckler, he is to pay fourpence ; if he sins with his tongue, or shouts or makes melody when others wish to study or sleep, or brings to table an unsheathed knife, or speaks English, or goes into the town or the fields unaccompanied by a fellow-student, he is fined a farthing ; if he comes in after 8 P.M. in winter or 9 P.M. in summer, he contracts a gate bill of a penny ; if he sleeps out, or puts up a friend for the night, without leave of his Principal, the fine is fourpence ; if he sleeps with another student in the Hall but not in his own bed, he pays a penny ; if he brings a stranger to a meal or a lecture or any other " actum communem " in the Hall, he is fined twopence ; if he is pugnacious and offensive and makes odious comparisons, he is to pay sixpence ;

if he attacks a fellow-member or a servant, the University has appointed penalties varying with the severity of the assault, and for a second offence he must be expelled. He has to obey his Principal much as members of a College obey their Head, and, in lieu of the pecuniary penalties, the Principal may flog him publicly on Saturday nights, even though his own master may certify that he has already corrected him, or declare his willingness to correct him, for his breaches of the statutes. The private master or tutor was, as Dr Rashdall suggests, probably a luxury of the rich boy, to whom his wealth might thus bring its own penalty.

It is startling to the modern mind to find University statutes and disciplinary regulations forbidding not only extravagant and unbecoming dress, but sometimes also the wearing of distinctive academic costume by undergraduates, for distinctive academic costume was the privilege of a graduate. The scholar wore ordinary clerical dress, unless the Founder of a College prescribed a special livery. The master had a *cappa* or cope, such as a Cambridge Vice-Chancellor wears on Degree Days, with a border and hood of minever, such as Oxford proctors still wear, and a *biretta* or square cap. In 1489, the insolence of many Oxford scholars had grown to such a pitch that they were not afraid to wear hoods in the fashion of masters, whereas bachelors, to their own damnation and the ruin of the University, were so regardless of their oaths as to wear hoods not lined throughout with fur. Penalties were prescribed for both kinds of offenders ; but though the Oxford undergraduate never succeeded in annexing the hood, he gradually acquired the *biretta*, which his successor of to-day is occasionally fined for not wearing. The modern gown or toga is explained by Dr Rashdall as derived from the robe or cassock which a medieval Master of Arts wore under his *cappa*.

The disciplinary regulations of fifteenth- and sixteenth-century Oxford may be paralleled from other universities. At Louvain there was a kind of proctorial walk undertaken by the University official known as the Promotor. On receiving three or four hours' notice from the Rector, the Promotor, with a staff of servants, perambulated the streets at night, and he and his " bulldogs " received a fine from anyone whom they apprehended. Offending students caught *in flagrante delicto* he conducted to the University prison, and others he reported to the Rector. " Notabiles personæ " might be incarcerated in a monastery incorporated with the University. Arms found upon anyone were forfeited. The Promotor was also the University gaoler, and was responsible for the safe custody of prisoners, and he might place in fetters dangerous prisoners or men accused of serious crimes. Interviews with captives had to take place in his presence ; male visitors had to give up their knives or other weapons before being admitted, and female visitors had to leave their cloaks behind them. Students were forbidden to walk in the streets at night after the bell of St Michael's Church had been rung at nine o'clock in winter, and ten o'clock in summer, unless they were accompanied by a doctor or a " gravis persona " and were bearing a torch or lantern. The list of offences at Louvain are much the same as elsewhere, but an eighteenth-century code of statutes specially prohibits bathing and skating. The laws against borrowing and lending were unusually strict, and no student under twenty-five years was allowed to sell books without the consent of his regent, the penalty for a sixteenth-century student in Arts being a public flogging in his own college.

At Leipsic, the University was generally responsible for the discipline, sometimes even when the offences had been committed in the colleges ; and a record of the proceedings of the Rector's Court from 1524 to 1588, which was published by Friedrich Zarncke, the learned historian of Leipsic, gives us a large variety of incidents of University life in sixteenth-century Germany. Leipsic possessed a University prison, and we find, in 1524, two students,

Philippus Josman and Erasmus Empedophillus, who had quarrelled, and insulted each other, sentenced to perform, in the prison, impositions for the Rector. Six or eight days' imprisonment is a frequent penalty for a drunken row. A college official brings to the Rector's Court in 1545 one of his pupils, John Ditz, who had lost much money by gambling. Ditz and one of his friends, Caspar Winckler, who had won six florins and some books from him, have already been flogged by their preceptors : they are now sentenced to imprisonment, but as the weather is very cold, they are to be released after one day's detention, and sent back to their preceptors to be flogged again. Their companions are sentenced to return any money, books or garments which they had won in gambling games. A student of the name of Valentine Muff complains to the Rector that his pedagogue has beaten and reproved him undeservedly : after an inquiry he is condemned to the rods " once and again." For throwing stones at windows a student is fined one florin in addition to the cost of replacing them. For grave moral offences fines of three florins are imposed, and the penalty is not infrequently reduced. A month's imprisonment is the alternative of the fine of three florins, but if the weather is cold, the culprit, who has been guilty of gross immorality, is let off with two florins. A drunken youth who meets some girls in the evening and tries to compel them to enter his college, is sentenced to five days' imprisonment, but is released on the intercession of the girls and many others. An attack on a servant with a knife is punished by forfeiture of the knife and a fine of half a florin, and a penalty of a florin (divided among the four victims) is inflicted for entering a house with arms and wounding the fingers of some of its inhabitants. A ruffian of noble birth, who had been guilty of gross immorality and of violence, declines to appear in the Rector's Court, and is duly sentenced to expulsion. But his father promises to satisfy the University and the injured party, and seven nobles write asking that he should be pardoned, and a compromise is made, by which he appears in court and pays a fine. For the University offence of having as an attendant a boy who is not enrolled, Valentine Leo is fined three florins, which were paid. "But since he appeared to be good and learned, and produced an excellent specimen of his singular erudition, and wrote learned verses and other compositions to the Rector and his assessors, by which he begged pardon and modestly purged his offence, and especially as a doctor, whose sons he taught, and others interceded for him, he easily procured that the florins should be returned to the doctor who had paid them for him."

The leniency of the punishments for grave moral offences, as contrasted with the strict insistance upon the lesser matters of the law, cannot fail to impress modern readers, but this is not a characteristic peculiar to Leipsic. Fines, and in the fifteenth and sixteenth centuries, whippings were frequently inflicted in all universities for violent attacks upon the person. Dr Rashdall quotes a case at Ingolstadt where a student who had killed another in a drunken bout was let off with the confiscation of his goods, and the penalty of expulsion was remitted ; and the eighteenth-century history of Corpus Christi College at Oxford supplies more recent instances of punishments which could scarcely be said to fit the crime.

The statutes of the French universities outside Paris and of the three medieval Scottish universities (St Andrews, Glasgow, and Aberdeen) supply many illustrations of the regulations we have noted elsewhere, but contain little that is unusual. St Andrews, which allowed hawking, forbade the dangerous game of football. The Faculty of Arts at Glasgow in 1532 issued an edict which has a curious resemblance to the Eton custom of " shirking." Reverence and filial fear were so important, said the masters, that no student was to meet the Rector, the Dean, or one of the Regents openly in the streets, by day or by night ; immediately he was observed he must slink away and escape as

best he could, and he must not be found again in the
streets without special leave. The penalty was a
public flogging. Similarly, even a lawful game must
not be played in the presence of a regent. Flogging
was a recognised penalty in all the Scottish universities ; it found its way into the system at St Andrews
and Glasgow, and was introduced at once at Aberdeen.
The early statutes of Aberdeen University (King's
College) unfortunately exist only in the form in which
they were edited in the seventeenth century. They include a rhymed series of rules for behaviour at table,
which, though post-medieval in date, give us some
clue to the table manners of the medieval students :—

> Majorem ne praevenia-
> Locum assignatum tenea-
> Mensae assignatae accumba-
> Manibus mundis nudis eda-
> Aperientes caput faciem ne obtega-
> Vultus hilares habea-
> Rite in convictu comeda-
> Sal cultello capia-
> Salinum ne dejicia-
> Manubrium haud aciem porriga-   tis
> Tribus cibos digitis prehenda-
> Cultro priusquam dente tera-
>
> .   .   .   .   .
>
> Ossa in orbem depona-
> Vel pavimentum jacia-
> Modeste omnia facia-
> Ossa si in convivas jacia-
> Nedum si illos vulnera-
> Ne queramini si vapula-

. . . .
Post haustum labia deterga- ⎫
Modicum, sed crebro biba- ⎪
. . . . ⎪
Os ante haustum evacua- ⎪
Ungues sordidulos fugia- ⎬ tis
. . . . ⎪
Ructantes terga reflecta- ⎪
Ne scalpatis cavea- ⎪
. . . . ⎪
Edere mementote ut viva- ⎪
Non vivere ut comed- ⎭

The Economist's accounts at Aberdeen have been
preserved for part of the year 1579, and show that the
food of a Scottish student, just after the medieval
period, consisted of white bread, oat bread, beef,
mutton, butter, small fish, partans (crabs), eggs,
a bill of fare certainly above the food of the lower
classes in Scotland at the time. The drinks mentioned are best ale, second ale, and beer. His
victuals interested the medieval student ; the conversation of two German students, as pictured in a
" students' guide " to Heidelberg (*cf.* p. 116), is
largely occupied with food. " The veal is soft and
bad : the calf cannot have seen its mother three
times : no one in my country would eat such stuff :
the drink is bitter." The little book shows us the
two students walking in the meadows, and when
they reach the Neckar, one dissuades the other
from bathing (a dangerous enterprise forbidden in

the statutes of some universities, including Louvain and Glasgow). They quarrel about a book, and nearly come to blows ; one complains that the other reported him to the master for sleeping in lecture. Both speak of the " lupi," the spies who reported students using the vernacular or visiting the kitchen. The " wolves " were part of the administrative machinery of a German University ; a statute of Leipsic in 1507 orders that, according to ancient custom, " lupi " or " signatores " be appointed to note the names of any student who talked German (" vulgarisantes ") that they might be fined in due course, the money being spent on feasts. One of the two Heidelberg students complains of having been given a " signum " or bad mark " pro sermone vulgariter prolato," and the other has been caught in the kitchen. They discuss their teachers ; one of them complains of a lecture because " nimis alta gravisque materia est." The little book gives, in some ways, a remarkable picture of German student life, with its interests and its temptations ; but it raises more problems than it solves, and affords a fresh illustration of the difficulty of attempting to recreate the life of the past.

CHAPTER VI

THE JOCUND ADVENT

THE medieval student began his academic career with an initiation ceremony which varied in different countries and at different dates, but which, so far as we know, always involved feasting and generally implied considerable personal discomfort. The designation, "bejaunus" or bajan, which signifies yellow-beak ("bec jaune"), seems to have been given almost everywhere to the freshman, and the custom of receiving the fledgeling into the academic society was, towards the close of the Middle Ages, no mere tradition of student etiquette, but an acknowledged and admitted academic rite. The tradition, which dates from very early times, and which has so many parallels outside University history, was so strong that the authorities seem to have deemed it wisest to accept it and to be content with trying to limit the expense and the "ragging" which it entailed.

We have no detailed knowledge of the initiation of the Parisian student, but a statute made by the University in 1342 proves that the two elements of bullying the new-comer and feasting at his expense were both involved in it. It relates that quarrels

frequently arise through the custom of seizing the
goods of simple scholars on the occasion of their
" bejaunia," and compelling them to expend on
feasting the money on which they intended to live.
Insults, blows, and other dangers are the general
results of the system, and the University orders that
no one shall exact money or anything else from
bajans except the " socii " with whom they live,
and they may take only a free-will offering. Bajans
are to reveal, under heavy penalties, the names of
any who molest them by word or blow, threatening
them or offering them insults. Offenders are to be
handed over to the Provost of Paris to be punished,
but not " ad penam sanguinis."

A fifteenth-century code of statutes of the Cistercian College at Paris (generally much less stern
than one would expect in a house of that severe
Order) refers to the traditions that had grown up
in the College about the initiation of a bajan, and
to the " insolentias et enormitates multas " which
accompanied their observance. The whole of the
ceremonies of initiation are therefore forbidden—
" omnes receptiones noviter venientium, quos
voluntaria opinione Bejanos nuncupare solent, cum
suis consequentiis, necnon bajulationes, fibrationes
. . . tam in capitulo, in dormitorio, in parvis
scholis, in jardinis, quam ubiubi, et tam de die
quam de nocte." With these evil customs is to go

the very name of the Abbas Bejanorum, and all
" vasa, munimenta, et instrumenta " used for these
ceremonies are to be given up. New-comers in
future are to be entrusted to the care of discreet
seniors, who will instruct them in the honourable
customs of the College, report their shortcomings
in church, in walks, and in games, supervise their
expenditure, and prevent their being overcharged
" pro jocundo adventu " or in other ways. So
strong was the tradition of the " jocund advent "
that it thus finds a place even in a reformer's constitution, and we find references to it elsewhere in
the statutes of Parisian colleges. An undated early
code, drawn up for the Treasurer's College, orders
the members to fulfil honestly their jocund advent
in accordance with the advice of their fellow students.
At Cornouaille, the new-comer is instructed to pay
for his jocund advent neither too meanly nor with
burdensome extravagance, but in accordance with
his rank and his means. At the College of Dainville
the expense of the bajan-hood is limited to a quart
of good wine (" ultra unum sextarium vini non
mediocris suis sociis pro novo suo ingressu seu
bejanno non solvat "). At the College of Cambray,
a bursar is to pay twenty shillings for utensils, and
to provide a pint of good wine for the fellows then
present in hall. Dr Rashdall quotes from the Register
of the Sorbonne an instance in which the Abbot of the

Bajans was fined eight shillings (to be expended in wine) because he had not fulfilled his duties in regard to the cleansing of the bajans by an aspersion of water on Innocents' Day. The bajans were not only washed, but carried in procession upon asses.

The statutes of the universities of Southern France, and especially of Avignon and Aix, give us some further information, and we possess a record of the proceedings at Avignon of the Court of the Abbot of the Bajans, referred to in the passage we have quoted from the regulations of the Cistercian College at Paris. Similar prohibitions occur in other College statutes.

At Avignon, the Confraternity of St Sebastian existed largely for the purgation of bajans and the control of the abuses which had grown up in connection with the jocund advent. One of its statutes, dated about 1450, orders that no novice, commonly called a bajan, shall be admitted to the purgation of his sins or take the honourable name of student until he has paid the sum of six *grossi* as entrance money to the Confraternity. There is also an annual subscription of three *grossi*, and the payment of these sums is to be enforced by the seizure of books, unless the defaulter can prove that he is unable to pay his entrance fee or subscription, as the case may be. The Prior and Councillors of the Fraternity have power to grant a dispensation on

the ground of poverty. After providing his feast,
and taking an oath, the bajan is to be admitted,
" jocose et benigne," is to lose his base name, and
after a year is to bear the honourable title of student.
Noblemen and beneficed clergy are to pay double.
The bajan is implored to comply with these regulations " corde hilarissimo," and his " socii " are adjured
to remember that they should not seek their own
things but the things of Christ, and should therefore
not spend on feasts anything over six *grossi* paid
by a bajan, but devote it to the honour of God and
St Sebastian. The Court of the Abbot of the
Bajans, at the College of Annecy, in the same University, throws a little more light on the actual ceremony
of purgation. The bajans are summoned into the
Abbot's Court, where each of them receives, *pro
forma*, a blow from a ferule. They all stand in the
Court, with uncovered heads and by themselves
(" Mundus ab immundo venit separandus "); under
the penalty of two blows they are required to keep
silence (" quia vox funesta in judiciis audiri non
debet.") The bajan who has patiently and honestly
served his time and is about to be purged, is given,
in parody of an Inception in the University, a
passage in the Institutes to expound, and his fellow-
bajans, under pain of two blows, have to dispute
with him. If he obtains licence, the two last-purged
bajans bring water " pro lavatione et purgatione."

H

The other rules of the Abbot's Court deal with the
duties to be performed by the youngest freshman
in Chapel (and at table if servants are lacking), and
order bajans to give place to seniors and not to go
near the fire in hall when seniors are present. No
one, either senior or freshman, is to apply the term
" Domine " to a bajan, and no freshman is to call
a senior man a bajan. The Court met twice a
week, and it could impose penalties upon senior
men as well as bajans, but corporal punishment is
threatened only against the " infectos et fetidis-
simos bejannos."

At Aix, a fifteenth-century code of statutes orders
every bajan to pay fees to the University, and to
give a feast to the Rector, the Treasurer, and the
Promotor. The Rector is to bring one scholar
with him, and the Promotor two, to help " ad pur-
gandum bejaunum," and the bajan is to invite a
bedel and others. Dispensations on the ground of
poverty could be obtained from the Rector, and
two or three freshmen might make their purgation
together, " cum infinitas est vitanda," even an
infinity of feasts is to be avoided. The Promotor
gives the first blow with a frying-pan, and the
scholars who help in the purgation are limited to
two or three blows each, since an infinity of blows
is also to be avoided. The Rector may remit a
portion of the penalty at the request of noble or

honourable ladies who happen to be present, for
it is useless to invite ladies if no remission is to be
obtained.   If the bajan is proud or troublesome,
the pleas of the ladies whom he has invited will not
avail ; he must have his three blows from each
of his purgators, without any mercy.   If a freshman failed to make his purgation within a month,
it was to take place " in studio sub libro super
anum " ; the choice between a book and a frying-
pan as a weapon of castigation is characteristic of
the solemn fooling of the jocund advent.   The
seizure of goods and of books, mentioned in some
of the statutes we have quoted, is frequently forbidden.   At Orleans the statutes prohibit leading
the bajan " ut ovis ad occisionem " to a tavern
to be forced to spend his money, and denounce the
custom as provocative of " ebrietates, turpiloquia,
lascivias, pernoctationes " and other evils.   They
also forbid the practice of compelling him to celebrate the jocund advent by seizing books, one or
more, or by exacting anything from him.   There are
numerous other references in French statutes, some
of which denounce the *bejaunia* as sufficiently expensive to deter men from coming to the University,
but details are disappointingly few.

The initiation of the bajan attained its highest
development in the German universities, where we
find the French conception of the bajan, as afflicted

with mortal sin and requiring purification, combined with the characteristic German conception of him as a wild animal who has to be tamed. His reformation was accomplished by the use of planes, augers, saws, pincers and other instruments suitable for removing horns, tusks and claws from a dangerous animal, and the Deposition, or "modus deponendi cornua iis qui in numerum studiosorum co-optari volunt," became a recognised University ceremony. The statutes attempt to check it, *e.g.* at Vienna the bajan is not to be oppressed with undue exactions or otherwise molested or insulted, and at Leipsic the insults are not to take the form of blows, stones, or water. At Prague, "those who lay down (deponent) their rustic manners and ignorance are to be treated more mildly and moderately than in recent years (1544), and their lips or other parts of their bodies are not to be defiled with filth or putrid and impure substances which produce sickness. But the Prague statute contemplates a Deposition ceremony in which the freshman is assumed to be a goat with horns to be removed. A black-letter handbook or manual for German students, consisting of dialogues or conversational Latin (much on the principle of tourists' conversational dictionaries), opens with a description of the preparations for a Deposition. The book, which has been reprinted in Zarncke's *Die Deutschen Universitäten im*

Mittelalter, is (from internal evidence) a picture of life at Heidelberg, but it is written in general terms.

The new-comer seeks out a master that he may be entered on the roll of the University and be absolved from his bajan-ship. " Are your parents rich ? " is one of the master's first questions, and he is told that they are moderately prosperous mechanics who are prepared to do the best for their son. The master takes him to the Rector to be admitted, and then asks him, " Where do you intend to have your ' deposition ' as a bajan ? " The boy leaves all arrangements in the master's hands, reminding him of his poverty, and it is agreed to invite three masters, two bachelors, and some friends of the master to the ceremony. With a warning that he must not be afraid if strangers come and insult him, for it is all part of the tradition of a bajan's advent, the master goes to make arrangements for the feast. Two youths, Camillus and Bartoldus, then arrive, and pretend to be greatly disturbed by a foul smell, so strong that it almost drives them from the room. Camillus prepares to go, but Bartoldus insists upon an investigation of the cause. Camillus then sees a monster of terrible aspect, with huge horns and teeth, a nose curved like the beak of an owl, wild eyes and threatening lips. " Let us flee," he says, " lest it attack us." Bartoldus then guesses that it is a bajan, a creature which Camillus has never seen, but of whose ferocity he has heard. The bold Bartoldus then addresses the bajan. " Domine Joannes," he says, " whence do you come ? Certainly you are a compatriot of mine, give me your hand." Joannes stretches out his hand, but is met with the indignant question, " Do you come to attack me with your nails ? Why do you sit down, wild ass ? Do you not see that masters are present, venerable men, in whose presence it becomes you to stand ? " Joannes stands, and is further insulted. His tormentors then affect to be sorry for him and make touching references to his mother's feelings (" Quid, si mater sciret, quae unice eum amat ? "), but relapse into abuse (O beane, O asine, O foetide hirce, O olens capra, O bufo, O cifra, O figura nihili, O tu omnino nihil). " What are we to do with him ? " says Camillus, and Bartoldus suggests the possibility of his reformation and admission into their society. But they must have a doctor. Camillus is famous and learned in the science of medicine, and can remove his horns, file down his teeth, cure his blindness, and shave his long and horrible beard. While he goes for the necessary instruments, Bartoldus tells the victim to cheer up, for he is about to be cured from every evil of mind and body, and to be admitted to the privileges of the University. Camillus returns with ointment, and they proceed to some horseplay which Joannes resists (Compesce eius impetus et ut equum intractatum ipsum illum constringe)." Tusks and teeth having been removed, the victim is supposed to be dying, and is made to confess to Bartoldus a list of crimes. His penance is to entertain his masters "largissima coena," not forgetting the doctor who has just healed him, and the confessor who has just heard his confession, for they also must be entertained " pingui refectione." But this confessor can only define the penance, he cannot give absolution, a right which belongs to the masters. Joannes is then taken to his master for the Deposition proper. Dr Rashdall describes the scene, from a rare sixteenth-century tract, which contains an illustration of a Deposition, and a defence of it by Luther, who justified his taking part in one of these ceremonies by giving it a moral and sym- bolical meaning. The bajan lies upon a table, under- going the planing of his tusks, " while a saw lies upon the ground, suggestive of the actual de-horning of the beast. The work itself and later apologies for the institution mention among the instruments of torture a comb and scissors for cutting the victim's hair, an *auriscalpium* for his ears, a knife for cutting his nails ; while the ceremony further appears to include the adornment of the youth's chin with a beard by means of burned cork or other pigment, and the administration, internal or external, of salt and wine."

In the English universities we have no trace of the " jocund advent " during the medieval period, but it is impossible to doubt that this kind of horseplay existed at Oxford and Cambridge. The statutes of New College refer to " that most vile and horrid sport of shaving beards " ; it was " wont to be practised on the night preceding the Inception of a Master of Arts," but the freshmen may have been the victims, as they were in similar ceremonies at the Feast of Fools in France. Antony à Wood, writing of his own undergraduate days in the middle of the seventeenth century, tells that charcoal fires were made in the Hall at Merton on Holy Days, from All Saints' Eve to Candlemas, and that

" at all these fires every night, which began to be made a little after five of the clock, the senior undergraduates would bring into the hall the juniors or freshmen between that time and six of the clock, there make them sit downe on a forme in the middle of the hall, joyning to the declaiming desk ; which done, every one in order was to speake some pretty apothegme, or make a jest or bull, or speake some eloquent nonsense, to make the company laugh. But if any of the freshmen came off dull, or not cleverly, some of the forward or pragmatised seniors would " tuck " them, that is, set the nail of their thumb to their

chin, just under the lower lipp, and by the help
of their other fingers under the chin, they would
give him a mark, which sometimes would produce
blood."

On Shrove Tuesday, 1648, Merton freshmen
entertained the other undergraduates to a brass pot
" full of cawdel." Wood, who was a freshman,
describes how

" every freshman according to seniority, was to
pluck off his gowne and band and if possible to
make himself look like a scoundrell. This done,
they conducted each other to the high table, and
there made to stand on a forme placed thereon ;
from whence they were to speak their speech with
an audible voice to the company ; which if well
done, the person that spoke it was to have a cup
of cawdle and no salted drink ; if indifferently,
some cawdle and some salted drink ; but if dull,
nothing was given to him but salted drink or salt
put in college beere, with tucks to boot. Afterwards when they were to be admitted into the
fraternity, the senior cook was to administer to
them an oath over an old shoe, part of which runs
thus : Item tu jurabis quod penniless bench (a
seat at Carfax) non visitabis' &c. The rest is
forgotten, and none there are now remembers it.
After which spoken with gravity, the Freshman
kist the shoe, put on his gown and band and took
his place among the seniors."

" This," says Wood, " was the way and custom
that had been used in the college, time out of mind,
to initiate the freshmen ; but between that time
and the restoration of K. Ch. 2 it was disused, and
now such a thing is absolutely forgotten." His
whole description, and especially the parody of the
master's oath not to visit Stamford, goes to show
that he was right in attributing the ceremonies to
remote antiquity, and there are indications that
the initiation of freshmen was practised elsewhere
in Oxford. Hearne speaks of similar customs
at Balliol and at Brasenose, and an eighteenth-
century editor of Wood asserts that " striking
traces " of the practice " may be found in many
societies in this place, and in some a very near
resemblance of it has been kept up till within these
few years." Our quotation from Wood may therefore serve to illustrate the treatment of the medieval
freshman at Oxford. We possess no details of the
jocund advent at Cambridge, but in the medieval
Scottish universities, where the name of bajan
still survives, there were relics of it within recent
times. At St Andrews, a feast of raisins was the
last survival of the bajan's " standing treat," and
attacks made by " Semis " (second year men) upon
a bajan class emerging from a lecture-room were an
enlivening feature of student life at Aberdeen up
to the end of the nineteenth century. The weapons

in use were notebooks, and the belabouring of Aberdeen bajans with these instruments may be historically connected with the chastisement which we have found in some of the medieval initiation ceremonies. It would be fanciful to connect the gown-tearing, which was also a feature of these attacks, with the assaults upon the Rector's robe at Bologna.

CHAPTER VII

TOWN AND GOWN

THE violence which marked medieval life as a whole
was not likely to be absent in towns where numbers
of young clerks were members of a corporation at
variance with the authorities of the city. University records are full of injuries done to masters and
students by the townsfolk, and of privileges and
immunities obtained from Pope or King or Bishop
at the expense of the burgesses. When a new
University was founded, it was sometimes taken for
granted that these conflicts must arise, and that
the townsmen were certain to be in the wrong.
Thus, when Duke Rudolf IV. founded the University
of Vienna in 1365, he provided beforehand for
such contingencies by ordaining that an attack on
a student leading to the loss of a limb or other
member of the body was to be punished by the
removal of the same member from the body of the
assailant, and that for a lesser injury the offender's
hand was to be wounded (" debet manus pugione
transfigi "). The criminal might redeem his person
by a fine of a hundred silver marks for a serious
injury and of forty marks for slighter damages, the

victim to receive half of the fine. Assailants of
students were not to have benefit of sanctuary.
Oxford history abounds in town and gown riots, the
most famous of which is the battle of St Scholastica's Day (10th February) 1354. The riot originated
in a tavern quarrel ; some clerks disapproved of the
wine at an inn near Carfax, and (in Antony Wood's
words) "the vintner giving them stubborn and
saucy language, they threw the wine and vessel
at his head." His friends urged the inn-keeper
"not to put up with the abuse," and rang the bell
of St Martin's Church. A mob at once assembled,
armed with bows and arrows and other weapons ;
they attacked every scholar who passed, and even
fired at the Chancellor when he attempted to allay
the tumult. The justly indignant Chancellor re-
torted by ringing St Mary's bell and a mob of
students assembled, also armed (in spite of many
statutes to the contrary). A battle royal raged till
nightfall, at which time the fray ceased, no one
scholar or townsman being killed or mortally
wounded or maimed." If the matter had ended
then, little would have been heard of the story,
but next day the townsmen stationed eighty armed
men in St Giles's Church, who sallied out upon
"certain scholars walking after dinner in Beaumont
killed one of them, and wounded others. A second
battle followed, in which the citizens, aided by some

countrymen, defeated the scholars, and ravaged their halls, slaying and wounding. Night interrupted their operations, but on the following day, " with hideous noises and clamours they came and invaded the scholars' houses . . . and those that resisted them and stood upon their defence (particularly some chaplains) they killed or else in a grievous sort wounded. . . . The crowns of some chaplains, that is, all the skin so far as the tonsure went, these diabolical imps flayed off in scorn of their clergy."

The injured University was fully avenged. The King granted it jurisdiction over the city, and, especially, control of the market, and the Bishop of Lincoln placed the townsmen under an interdict which was removed only on condition that the Mayor and Bailiffs, for the time being, and " three-score of the chiefest Burghers, should personally appear " every St Scholastica's Day in St Mary's Church, to attend a mass for the souls of the slain. The tradition that they were to wear halters or silken cords has no authority, but they were each " to offer at the altar one penny, of which oblation forty pence should be distributed to forty poor scholars of the University." The custom, with some modifications, survived the Reformation, and it was not till the nineteenth century that the Mayor of Oxford ceased to have cause to regret the battle of St Scholastica's Day.

The accounts of St Scholastica's Day and of most other riots which have come down to us are written from the standpoint of the scholars, but the records of the city of Oxford give less detailed but not less credible instances of assaults by members of the University. On the eve of St John Baptist's Day in 1306, for example, the tailors of Oxford were celebrating Midsummer " cum Cytharis Viellis et aliis diversis instrumentis." After midnight, they went out " de shoppis suis " and danced and sang in the streets. A clerk, irritated by the noise, attacked them with a drawn sword, wounded one of them, and was himself mortally wounded in the skirmish. Of twenty-nine coroners' inquests which have been preserved for the period 1297-1322, thirteen are murders committed by scholars. Attacks on townsmen were not mere undergraduate follies, but were countenanced and even led by officials of the University, *e.g.* on a March night in 1526 one of the proctors " sate uppon a blocke in the streete afore the shoppe of one Robert Jermyns, a barber, havinge a pole axe in his hand, a black cloake on his backe, and a hatt on his head," and organised a riot in which many townsmen were " striken downe and sore beaten." Citizens' houses were attacked and " the saide Proctour and his company . . . called for fire," threatening to burn the houses, and insulting the inmates with opprobrious names. When such an incident as this was possible, it was of little use for the University to issue regulations or even to punish less exalted sinners, and the town must have suffered much from the outrages of scholars and of the "chamber-dekens" or pretended scholars of the University, who were responsible for much of the mischief. At Paris things became so bad that the Parlement had to issue a series of police regulations to suppress the bands of scholars, or pretended scholars, who wandered about the streets at night, disguised and armed. They attacked passers-by, and if they were wounded in the affray, their medical friends, we are told, dressed their wounds, so that they eluded discovery in the morning. The history of every University town provides instances of street con-flicts—the records of Orleans and Toulouse abound in them—but we must be content with a tale from Leipsic.

The pages of the " Acta Rectorum " at Leipsic are full of illustrations of the wilder side of student life, from which we extract the story of one un-happy year. The year 1545 opened very badly, says the " Rector's Chronicle," with three homicides. On Holy Innocents' Day, a bachelor was murdered by a skinner in a street riot, and the murderer, though he was seen by some respectable citizens, was allowed to escape. A student who killed a man on the night of the Sunday after the Epiphany was punished by the University in accordance with its statutes (*i.e.* by imprisonment for life in the bishop's prison). The third murder was that of a young bachelor who was walking outside the city, when two sons of rustics in the neighbourhood fell on him and killed him. Their names were known, but the city authorities refused to take action, and the populace, believing that they would not be punished, pursued the members of the University with continued insults and threats. After an unusually serious attack *cum bombardis*, (in which, " by the divine clemency," a young mechanic was wounded), the University, failing to obtain redress, appealed to Prince Maurice of Saxony, who promised to protect the University. A conference between the University and the city authorities took place, and edicts against carrying arms were published, but the skinners immediately indulged in another outrage. One of them, Hans von Buntzell, on Whitsunday, attacked, with a drawn sword, the son of a doctor of medicine, " a youth (as all agree) most guiltless," and wounded him in the arm, and if another student had not unexpectedly appeared, " would without doubt have killed this excellent boy." The criminal was pursued to the house of a skinner called Meysen, where he took refuge. The city authorities, inspired by the

I

Prince's intervention, offered to impose three alternative sentences, and the University was asked to say whether Hans von Buntzell should lose one of his hands, or be publicly whipped and banished for ten years, or should have a certain stigma (" quod esset manus amittendae signum ") burned in his hand and be banished. The University replied that it was for the city to carry out the commands of the Prince, and declined to select the penalty. On the following Monday a scaffold was erected in the market-place, on which were placed rods and a knife for cutting off the hand, " which apparatus was thought by the skinners to be much too fierce and cruel, and a concourse began from all parts, composed not of skinners alone, but of mechanics of every kind, interceding with the Council for the criminal." The pleadings of the multitude gained the day, and all the preparations were removed from the market-place amid the murmurs of the students. After supper, three senior members of the skinners came to the Rector, begging for a commutation of the punishment, and offering to beat Hans themselves in presence of representatives of the University and the Town Council, with greater ferocity than the public executioner could do if he were to whip him three times in public. The Rector replied that he must consult the University, and the proposal was thrown out in

Congregation. On the Saturday after the Feast of Trinity, the stigma was burned on the criminal's hand, and as a necessary consequence he was banished.

Town riots do not complete the tale of violence. There were struggles with Jews, and a Jewish row at Oxford in 1268 resulted in the erection of a cross with the following inscription :—

> Quis meus auctor erat ? Judaei. Quomodo ? Sumptu
> Quis jussit ? Regnans. Quo procurante ? Magistri.
> Cur ? Cruce pro fracta ligni. Quo tempore ? Festo
> Ascensus Domini. Quis est locus ? Hic ubi sisto.

Clerks' enemies were not always beyond their own household. The history of Paris, the earlier history of Oxford, and the record of many another University give us instances of mortal combats between the Nations. The scholars of Paris, in the thirteenth and fourteenth centuries, had to face the mortal enmity of the monks of the Abbey of St Germain, the meadow in front of which was claimed by the Faculty of Arts. The sight of Paris students walking or playing on the Pré-aux-clercs had much the same effect upon the Abbot and monks as the famous donkeys had upon the strong-minded aunt of David Copperfield, but the measures they took for suppressing the nuisance were less exactly proportioned to the offence. One summer day in 1278, masters and scholars went for recreation to the meadow, when the Abbot sent out armed servants and retainers of the monastery to attack them. They came shouting " Ad mortem clericorum," death to the clerks, " verbis crudelibus, *ad mortem ad mortem*, inhumaniter pluries repetitis." A " famous Bachelor of Arts " and other clerks were seriously wounded and thrown into horrible dungeons ; another victim lost an eye. The retreat into the city was cut off, and fugitives were pursued far into the country. Blood flowed freely, and the scholars who escaped returned to their halls with broken heads and limbs and their clothes torn to fragments. Some of the victims died of their wounds, and the monks were punished by King and Pope, the Abbot being pensioned off and the Abbey compelled to endow two chaplains to say masses for scholars. Forty years later the University had again to appeal to the Pope to avenge assaults by retainers of the Abbey upon scholars who were fishing in the moat outside the Abbey walls. The monks, of course, may have given a different version of the incidents.

CHAPTER VIII

SUBJECTS OF STUDY, LECTURES AND EXAMINATIONS

THE student of a medieval University was, as we have seen, expected to converse in Latin, and all instruction was given in that language. It was therefore essential that, before entering on the University curriculum, he should have a competent knowledge of Latin. College founders attempted to secure this in various ways, sometimes by an examination (*e.g.* at the College of Cornouaille, at Paris, no one was admitted a bursar until he was examined and found to be able to read), and sometimes by making provision for young boys to be taught by a master of grammar. The Founder of New College met the difficulty by the foundation of Winchester College, at which all Wykehamists (except the earliest members of New College) were to be thoroughly grounded in Latin. It was more difficult for a University to insist upon such a test, but, in 1328, the University of Paris had ordered that before a youth was admitted to the privileges of " scholarity " or studentship, he must appear before the Rector and make his own application in continuous Latin, without any French words. Formulae for this purpose would, doubtless, soon be invented and handed down by tradition, and the precaution cannot have been of much practical value. There were plenty of grammar schools in the Middle Ages, and a clever boy was likely to find a patron and a place of education in the neighbourhood of his home. The grammar schools in University towns had therefore originally no special importance, but many of the undergraduates who came up at thirteen or fourteen required some training such as William of Waynflete provided for his younger demies in connexion with the Grammar School which he attached to Magdalen, or such as Walter de Merton considered desirable when he ordained that there should be a Master of Grammar in his College to teach the poor boys, and that their seniors were to go to him in any difficulty without any false shame (" absque rubore "). Many universities extended certain privileges to boys studying grammar, by placing their names on matriculation rolls, though such matriculation was not part of the curriculum for a degree. Masters in Grammar were frequently, but not necessarily, University graduates ; at Paris there were grammar mistresses as well as grammar masters. The connexion between the grammar schools and the University was exceptionally close at Oxford and Cambridge, where degrees in grammar came to be given.   The University of Oxford early legislated for " inceptors " who were taking degrees in grammar, and ordered the grammar masters who were graduates to enrol, *pro forma*, the names of pupils of non-graduates, and to compel non-graduate masters to obey the regulations of the University.   A meeting of the grammar masters twice a term for discussions about their subject and the method of teaching it was also ordered by the University, which ultimately succeeded in wresting the right of licensing grammar masters from the Archdeacon or other official to whom it naturally belonged.   A fourteenth-century code of statutes for the Oxford grammar schools orders the appointment of two Masters of Arts to superintend them, and gives some minute instructions about the teaching.   Grammar masters are to set verses and compositions, to be brought next day for correction ;   and they are to be specially careful to see that the younger boys can recognise the different parts of speech and parse them accurately.   In choosing books to read with their pupils, they are to avoid the books of Ovid " de Arte Amandi " and similar works.   Boys are to be taught to construe in French as well as in English, lest they be ignorant of the French tongue.   The study of French was not confined to the grammar boys :   the University recognised the wisdom of learning a

language necessary for composing charters, holding
lay-courts, and pleading in the English fashion, and
lectures in French were permitted at any hour
that did not interfere with the regular teaching of
Arts subjects. Such lectures were under the control of the superintendents of the grammar masters.

The degrees which Oxford and Cambridge conferred in Grammar did not involve residence or
entitle the recipients to a vote in Convocation ;
but the conferment was accompanied by ceremonies
which were almost parodies of the solemn proceedings of graduation or inception in a recognised
Faculty, a birch taking the place of a book as a
symbol of the power and authority entrusted to the
graduand. A sixteenth-century Esquire Bedel of
Cambridge left, for the benefit of his successors,
details of the form for the " enteryng of a Master
in Gramer." The " Father " of the Faculty of
Grammar (at Cambridge the mysterious individual
known as the " Master of Glomery ") brought his
" sons " to St Mary's Church for eight o'clock mass.
" When mass is done, fyrst shall begynne the acte
in Gramer. The Father shall have hys sete made
before the Stage for Physyke (one of the platforms
erected in the church for doctors of the different
faculties, etc.) and shall sytte alofte under the stage
for Physyke. The Proctour shall say, Incipiatis.
When the Father hath argyude as shall plese the

Proctour, the Bedeyll in Arte shall bring the Master
of Gramer to the Vyce-chancelar, delyveryng hym
a Palmer wyth a Rodde, whych the Vyce-chancelar
shall gyve to the seyde Master in Gramer, and so
create hym Master.   Then shall the Bedell purvay
for every master in Gramer a shrewde Boy, whom
the master in Gramer shall bete openlye in the
Scolys, and the master in Gramer shall give the
Boy a Grote for Hys Labour, and another Grote
to hym that provydeth the Rode and the Palmer
&c. de singulis.   And thus endythe the Acte in
that Facultye."   We know of the existence of
similar ceremonies at Oxford.   " Had the ambition
to take these degrees in Grammar been widely
diffused," says Dr Rashdall, " the demand for
whipping boys might have pressed rather hardly
upon the youth of Oxford ; but very few of them
are mentioned in the University Register."

The basis of the medieval curriculum in Arts is to
be found in the Seven Liberal Arts of the Dark Ages,
divided into the *Trivium* (Grammar, Rhetoric and
Dialectic) and the *Quadrivium* (Music, Arithmetic,
Geometry and Astronomy).   The *Quadrivium* was
of comparatively little importance ; Geometry and
Music received small attention ; and Arithmetic,
and Astronomy were at first chiefly useful for
finding the date of Easter ; but the introduction of
mathematical learning from Arabian sources in

the thirteenth century greatly increased the scope of Geometry and Arithmetic, and added the study of Algebra.

The Grammar taught in the universities assumed a knowledge of such a text-book as that of Alexander de Villa Dei, and consisted of an analysis of the systems of popular grammarians, based on the section *De barbarismo* in the *Ars Grammatica* of Ælius Donatus, a fourth-century grammarian, whose work became universally used throughout Europe. Latin poets were read in the grammar schools, and served for grammatical and philological expositions in the universities, and the study of Rhetoric depended largely on the treatises of Cicero. The " Dialectic " of the *Trivium* was the real interest of the medieval student among the ancient seven subjects, but the curriculum in Arts came to include also the three Philosophies, Physical, Moral, and Metaphysical. The arms of the University of Oxford consist of a book with seven clasps surrounded by three crowns, the clasps representing the seven Liberal Arts and the crowns the three Philosophies. The universities were schools of philosophy, mental and physical, and the attention of students in Arts was chiefly directed to the logic, metaphysics, physics, and ethics of Aristotle. Up to the twelfth century, Aristotle was known only through the translations into Latin of the sections of the *Organon*, entitled *De Interpretatione* and *Categoriae*, and through the logical works of Boethius. In the twelfth and thirteenth centuries the range of medieval studies was greatly enlarged by the introduction of other works of Aristotle from translations partly from the Arabic and partly direct from the Greek. The conservatism of the University of Paris at first forbade the study of the new Aristotle, but it soon became universal in the medieval universities. In addition to the works of Aristotle, as they were known in the Middle Ages, medieval students read such books as Porphyry's *Isagoge*, or Introduction to Aristotle; the criticism of Aristotle's *Categories*, by Gilbert de la Porrée, known as the *Sex Principia*; the *Summulae Logicales*, a semi-grammatical, semi-logical treatise by Petrus Hispanus (Pope John XXI.); the *Parva Logicalia* of Marsilius of Inghen; the *Labyrinthus* and *Grecismus* of Eberhard; the Scriptural commentaries of Nicolaus de Lyra; the *Tractatus de Sphaera*, an astronomical work by a thirteenth-century Scotsman, John Holywood (Joannes de Sacro Bosco); and they also studied Priscian, Donatus, Boethius, Euclid, and Ptolemy. In 1431 the *Nova Rhetorica* of Cicero, the *Metamorphoses* of Ovid, and the works of Virgil were prescribed at Oxford as alternatives to the fourth book of the *Topica* of Boethius. By the end of the century

Humanism had found a place in the universities, and sixteenth - century colleges at Oxford and Cambridge provided for the study of the literatures of Greece and Rome. In Scotland the medieval teaching of Aristotle reigned supreme in all its three universities until the appointment of Andrew Melville as Principal at Glasgow in 1574, and in 1580 he had some difficulty in persuading the masters at St Andrews to " peruse Aristotle in his ain language."

Lectures were either " ordinary " or " cursory," a distinction which, as Dr Rashdall has shown, corresponded to the " ordinary " and " extra-ordinary " lectures at Bologna. The ordinary lectures were the statutable exercises appointed by the Faculty, and delivered by its properly accredited teachers in the hours of the morning, which were sacred to the prelections of the masters. Cursory lectures were delivered in the afternoon, frequently by bachelors ; but as College teaching became more important than the lectures given in the Schools, the distinction gradually disappeared. Ordinary lectures were delivered " solemniter " and involved a slow and methodical analysis of the book. The statutes of Vienna prescribe that no master shall read more than one chapter of the text " ante quaestionem vel etiam quaestione expedita." Various references in College and University statutes show that the cursory lecture was not regarded as the full equivalent of an ordinary lecture. At Oxford, attendance on a lecture on the books or any book of the Metaphysics, or on the Physics, or the Ethics, was not to count for a degree, except in the case of a book largely dealing with the opinions of the ancients. The third and fourth books of the Metaphysics were excepted from the rule, "they being usually read cursorily, that the ordinary reading of the other books might proceed more rapidly." The cursory lecture was clearly beloved of the pupil, for Oxford grammar masters are reproved for lecturing "cursorie" instead of "ordinarie" for the sake of gain; and at Vienna, the tariff for cursory lectures is double that for ordinary lectures. At Paris the books of Aristotle de Dialectica were to be read "ordinarie et non ad cursum," and students of medicine had to read certain books "semel ordinarie, bis cursorie." The statutes of Heidelberg contrast "cursorie" with "extense." In the Faculty of Canon Law there was an additional distinction, the ordinary lecture being generally restricted to the Decretum; at Oxford, the book of Decretals is to be read at the morning hours at which the doctors of law are wont to deliver ordinary lectures, and at Vienna the doctors are forbidden to read anything but the Decretals in the morning at ordinary lectures.

The instructions given to the Vienna doctors of law illustrate the thoroughness of the medieval lecture in all faculties. They are first to state the case carefully, then to read the text, then to re-state the case, then to remark on " notabilia," and then to discuss questions arising out of the subject, and finally, to deal with the Glosses. So, at Oxford, the Masters in Arts are to read the books on logic and the philosophies " rite," with the necessary and adequate exposition of the text, and with questions and arguments pertinent to the subject-matter.

A problem, still unsolved, about the methods of lecturing disturbed the minds of the Parisian masters. Were they to dictate lectures or to speak so fast that their pupils could not commit their words to writing ? From the standpoint of teachers who delivered frequent lectures, all of the same type, and on a few set books, it was probably desirable that there should not be opportunities of possessing such copies of a professor's lectures as used to circulate, not many years ago, in Scottish and in German universities. In 1229 the Faculty of Arts at Paris made a statute on the methods of lecturing. It explains that there are two ways of reading books in the liberal arts. The masters of philosophy may deliver their expositions from their chairs so rapidly that, although the minds of their audience may grasp their meaning, their hands cannot write it down. This, they say, was the custom in other faculties. The other way is to speak so slowly that their hearers can take down what they say. On mature reflection, the Faculty has decided that the former is the better way, and henceforth in any lecture, ordinary or cursory, or in any disputation or other manner of teaching, the master is to speak as in delivering a speech, and as if no one were writing in his presence. A lecturer who breaks the new rule is to be suspended for a year, and if the students showed their dislike to it, by shouting, hissing, groaning, or throwing stones, they were to be sent down for a year. More than two hundred years later, in 1452, the statute was rescinded by Cardinal Estoutville, but it was probably never operative. Estoutville permitted either method of lecturing, and contented himself with forbidding lecturers to use questions and lectures which were not of their own composition, or to deliver their lectures (however good) to be read by one of their scholars as a deputy. He instructs the masters to lecture regularly according to the statutes and to explain the text of Aristotle, "de puncto in punctum," and, holding that fear and reverence are the life-blood of scholastic discipline, he repeats an injunction which we find in 1336, that the students in Arts are to sit not on benches or raised seats, but on the floor, "ut occasio superbiae a juvenibus secludatur." The name of the street in which lectures were given, Vicus Stramineus, is said to have been derived from the straw on which the students sat. The question whether lectures should be committed to writing or not, troubled the masters of other universities besides Paris, and the statutes of the College de Verdale at Toulouse accept, in 1337, the view taken at Paris a hundred years earlier. Since study is a vehement application of the mind, and requires the whole man, the scholars are forbidden to fatigue themselves with too many lectures—not more than two or three a day—and in lecture they are not to take down the lecturer's words, nor, trusting in writings of this kind, to blunt their " proprium intellectum." In the Schools, they must not use " incausta " or pencils except for correcting a book, etc. And what they have been able to retain in their memory they must meditate on without delay.

The insistence on meditation was a useful educational method, but as teaching became more organised, the student was not left without guidance in his meditations. The help which he received outside lectures was given in Repetitions or Resumptions. The procedure at Repetitions may be illustrated from the statutes of the College of Dainville at Paris : " We ordain that all bursars in grammar and philosophy speak the Latin tongue, and that those who hear the same book ordinarily and cursorily shall attend one and the same master (namely, one whom the master [of the College] assigns to them), and after the lecture they shall return home and meet in one place to repeat the lecture. One after another shall repeat the whole lecture, so that each of them may know it well, and the less advanced shall be bound daily to repeat the lectures to the more proficient." A later code of the same College provides that " All who study humane letters shall, on every day of the schools read in the morning a composition, that is a speech in Latin, Greek or the vernacular, to their master, being prepared to expound the writer or historian who is being read in daily lecture in their schools. At the end of the week, that is on Friday or Saturday, they shall show up to their master a résumé of all the lectures they have learned that week, and every day before they go to the schools they shall be bound to make repetitions to one of the philosophers or of the theologians whom the [College] master shall choose for this work." At Louvain, the time between 5 A.M. and the first lecture (about seven) was spent in studying the lesson that the students might better understand the lecture ; after hearing it, they returned to their own rooms to revise it and commit it to memory. After dinner, their books

K

were placed on a table, and all the scholars of one Faculty repeated their lesson and answered questions. A similar performance took place in the two hours before supper. After supper, the tutor treated them for half an hour to a "jocum honestum," and before sending them to bed gave them a light and pleasant disputation. The disputation was a preparation for the disputations which formed part of what we should now term the degree examinations. A thesis was propounded, attacked, and defended (" impugned and propugned ") with the proper forms of syllogistic reasoning.

The teaching, both in lectures and in disputations, was originally University teaching, and the younger Masters of Arts, the " necessary regents," were bound to stay up for some years and lecture in the Schools. They were paid by their scholars, and the original meaning of the word " Collections," still in frequent use at Oxford, is traditionally supposed to be found in the payments made for lectures at the end of each term. Thus, at Oxford, a student paid threepence a term (one shilling a year) to his regent for lectures in Logic, and fourpence a term for lectures in Natural Philosophy. The system was not a satisfactory one, and alike in Paris, in Oxford, and in Cambridge, it succumbed to the growth of College teaching. The Head of a Parisian College, from the first, superintended the studies of the scholars, and, although this duty was not required of an Oxford or Cambridge Head, provision was gradually made in the statutes of English colleges for the instruction of the junior members by their seniors. The first important step in this direction was taken by William of Wykeham, who ordered special payment to be made by the College to Fellows who undertook the tuition of the younger Fellows. His example was followed in this, as in other matters, by subsequent founders both at Oxford and at Cambridge, and gradually University teaching was, in the Faculty of Arts, almost entirely superseded by College tuition. In other universities, lectures continued to be given by University officials.

The medieval undergraduates had a tendency to "rag" in lectures, a tradition which is almost unknown at Oxford and Cambridge, but which persisted till quite recent times in the Scottish universities. Prohibitions of noise and disturbance in lecture-rooms abound in all statutes. At Vienna, students in Arts are exhorted to behave like young ladies (more virginum) and to refrain from laughter, murmurs, and hisses, and from tearing down the schedules in which the masters give notice of their lectures. At Prague, also, the conduc of young ladies was held up as a model for the student at lecture, and, at Angers, students who hissed in contempt of a doctor were to be expelled.

The career of a student was divided into two parts by his "Determination," a ceremony which is the origin of the Bachelor's degree. At Paris, where, at all events in the earlier period of its history, examinations were real, the "Determination" was preceded by "Responsions," and no candidate was admitted to determine until he had satisfied a Regent Master in the Schools, in public, "de Questione respondens." The determination itself was a public disputation, after which the determiner might wear the bachelor's "cappa" and lecture on the Organon. He continued his attendance on the lectures in the Schools up to the time of his "Inception" as a master. The Inception was preceded by an examination for licence and by a disputation known as the Quodlibetica, at which the subject was chosen by the candidate. The bachelor who was successful in obtaining the Chancellor's licence proceeded to the ceremony of Inception, and received his master's *biretta*.

The stringency of examinations varied in different universities and at different times. The proportion of successful candidates seems to have been everywhere very large, and in some universities rejection must have been almost unknown. We do find references to disappointed candidates, *e.g.* at Caen, where medical students who have been "ploughed" have to take an oath not to bring "malum vel damnum" upon the examiners. But even at Louvain, where the examination system was fully developed in the Middle Ages, and where there were class lists in the fifteenth century (the classes being distinguished as *Rigorosi*, *Transibiles*, and *Gratiosi*), failure was regarded as an exceptional event ("si autem, quod absit, aliqui inveniantur simpliciter gratiosi seu refutabiles, erunt de quarto ordine "). The regulations for examinations at Louvain prescribe that the examiners are not to ask disturbing questions (" animo turbandi aut confundendi promovendos ") and forbid unfair treatment of pupils of particular masters and frivolous or useless questions ; although at his Quodlibeticum, the bachelor might indulge in " jocosas questiones ad auditorii recreationem." The element of display implied in the last quotation was never absent from medieval examinations, and at Oxford, there seems to have been little besides this ceremonial element. A candidate had to prove that he had complied with the regulations about attendance at lectures, etc., and to obtain evidence of fitness from a number of masters. A bachelor had to dispute several times with a master, and these disputations, which were held at the Augustinian Convent, came to be known as " doing Austins." The medieval system, as it lingered at Oxford in the close of the eighteenth century, is thus described by Vicesimus Knox :—

" The youth whose heart pants for the honour of a Bachelor of Arts degree must wait patiently till near four years have revolved. . . . He is obliged during this period, once to oppose and once to respond. . . . This opposing and responding is termed, in the cant of the place, *doing generals*. Two boys or men, as they call themselves, agree to *do generals* together. The first step in this mighty work is to procure arguments. These are always handed down, from generation to generation, on long slips of paper, and consist of foolish syllogisms on foolish subjects, of the foundation or significance of which the respondent and opponent seldom know more than an infant in swaddling cloaths. The next step is to go for a *liceat* to one of the petty officers, called the Regent-Master of the Schools, who subscribes his name to the questions and receives sixpence as his fee. When the important day arrives, the two doughty disputants go into a large dusty room, full of dirt and cobwebs. . . . Here they sit in mean desks, opposite to each other from one o'clock till three. Not once in a hundred times does any officer enter ; and, if he does, he hears a syllogism or two, and then makes a bow, and departs, as he came and remained, in solemn silence. The disputants then return to the amusement of cutting the desks, carving their names, or reading Sterne's Sentimental Journey, or some other edifying novel. When the exercise is duly performed by both parties, they have a right to the title and insignia of *Sophs* : but not

before they have been formally *created* by one
of the regent-masters, before whom they kneel,
while he lays a volume of Aristotle's works on
their heads, and puts on a hood, a piece of black
crape, hanging from their necks, and down to
their heels. . . . There remain only one or two
trifling forms, and another disputation almost
exactly similar to *doing generals*, but called
answering under bachelor previous to the awful
examination. Every candidate is obliged to be
examined in the whole circle of the sciences by
three masters of arts *of his own choice*. . . .
Schemes, as they are called, or little books con-
taining forty or fifty questions on each science,
are handed down from age to age, from one to
another. The candidate employs three or four
days in learning these by heart, and the examiners,
having done the same before him, know what
questions to ask, and so all goes on smoothly.
When the candidate has displayed his universal
knowledge of the sciences, he is to display his
skill in philology. One of the masters therefore asks him to construe a passage in some Greek
or Latin classic, which he does with no interruption, just as he pleases, and as well as he can.
The statutes next require that he should translate
familiar English phrases into Latin. And now
is the time when the masters show their wit and
jocularity. . . . This familiarity, however,
only takes place when the examiners are pot-
companions of the candidate, which indeed is
usually the case ; for it is reckoned good manage-

ment to get acquainted with two or three jolly young masters of arts, and supply them well with port previously to the examination. If the vice-chancellor and proctors happen to enter the school, a very uncommon event, then a little solemnity is put on. . . . As neither the officer, nor anyone else, usually enters the room (for it is reckoned very *ungenteel*), the examiners and the candidates often converse on the last drinking-bout, or on horses, or read the newspapers or a novel."

The supply of port was the eighteenth-century relic of the feasts which used to accompany Determination and Inception, and with which so many sumptuary regulations of colleges and universities are concerned. There is a reference to a Determining Feast in the Paston Letters, in which the ill-fated Walter Paston, writing in the summer of 1479, a few weeks before his premature death, says to his brother : " And yf ye wyl know what day I was mead Baschyler, I was maad on Fryday was sevynyth, and I mad my fest on the Munday after. I was promysyd venyson ageyn my fest of my Lady Harcort, and of a noder man to, but I was desevyd of both ; but my gestes hewld them plesyd with such mete as they had, blyssyd be God. Hoo have yeo in Hys keeping. Wretyn at Oxon, on the Wedenys day next after Seynt Peter."

A few glimpses of the life of this fifteenth-century Oxonian may conclude our survey. Walter Paston had been sent to Oxford in 1473, under the charge of a priest called James Gloys. His mother did not wish him to associate too closely with the son of their neighbour, Thomas Holler. " I wold," she says, " Walter schuld be copilet with a better than Holler son is . . . howe be it I wold not that he schuld make never the lesse of hym, by cause he is his contre man and neghbour." The boy was instructed to " doo welle, lerne well, and be of good rewle and disposycion," and Gloys was asked to " bydde hym that he be not to hasty of takyng of orderes that schuld bynd him." To take Orders under twenty-three years of age might lead, in Margaret Paston's opinion, to repentance at leisure, and " I will love hym better to be a good secular man than to be a lewit priest." We next hear of Walter in May 1478 when he writes to his mother recommending himself to her " good moderchypp," and asking for money. He has received £5, 16s. 6d., and his expenses amount to £6, 5s. 5d. " That comth over the reseytys in my exspenses I have borrowed of Master Edmund and yt draweth to 8 shillings." He might have applied for a loan to one of the " chests " which benevolent donors had founded for such emergencies, depositing some article of value, and receiving a temporary loan : but he pre-

ferred to borrow from his new tutor, Edmund Alyard.
By March 1479, Alyard was able to reassure the
anxious mother about her boy's choice of a career ;
he was to go to law, taking his Bachelor's degree in
Arts at Midsummer. His brother, Sir John, who
was staying at the George at Paul's Wharf in London,
intended to be present at the ceremony, but his
letter miscarried : " Martin Brown had that same
tyme mysch mony in a bage, so that he durst not
bryng yt with hym, and that same letter was in that
same bage, and he had forgete to take owt the
letter, and he sent all togeder by London, so that
yt was the next day after that I was maad Bachyler
or than the letter cam, and so the fawt was not in
me." This is the last we hear of Walter Paston.
On his way home, on the 18th August 1479, he died
at Norwich, after a short illness. He left a number
of " togae " to his Oxford friends, including Robert
Holler, the son of his Norfolk neighbour, to whom
he also bequeathed " unum pulvinar vocatum *le
bolstar.*" The rest of his Oxford goods he left to
Alyard, but his sheep and his lands to his own
family. The cost of his illness and funeral amounted
to about thirty shillings. No books are mentioned
in the will ; possibly they were sold for his inception
feast, or he may never have possessed any. As a
junior student, he would not have been allowed
to use the great library which Humphrey of Glou-

cester had presented to the University ; but there were smaller libraries to which he might have access, for books were sometimes chained up in St Mary's Church that scholars might read them.

SELECTED BIBLIOGRAPHY

Savigny : Geschichte der römischen Rechts im Mittelalter. (Heidelberg, 1834.)

Sir William Hamilton : Discussions on Philosophy and Literature, Education, and University Reform. (London, 1852.)

Denifle : Die Entstehung der Universitäten des Mittelalters bis 1400. (Berlin, 1885.)

Rashdall : The Universities of Europe in the Middle Ages. (Oxford, 1895.)

Kaufmann : Geschichte der Deutschen Universitäten. (Stuttgart, 1888.)

Article on Universities in the *Encyclopædia Britannica*.

Archiv fur Lit. u. Kirchengeschichte des Mittelalters. Jurist Statutes of Padua (1331) in vol. vi. ; Salamanca documents in vol. v.

Malagola : Statuti della università e dei collegi dello studio bolognese. (Bologna, 1888.)

Denifle and Chatelain : Chartularium Universitatis Parisiensis. (Paris, 1889-1897.)

(Many of the statutes of the Colleges of Paris will be found scattered through Felibien : Histoire de la Ville de Paris. Paris, 1725.)

Antony Wood : History and Antiquities of the University of Oxford. (Ed. Gutch. Oxford, 1792-6.)

―――― History and Antiquities of the Colleges and Halls in the University of Oxford. (Ed. Gutch. Oxford, 1786.)

Anstey : Munimenta Academica. (Rolls Series, 1868.)

Statutes of the Colleges of Oxford. (London, 1853.)

Clark : The Colleges of Oxford. (London, 1892.)

(The best account of Oxford will be found in vol. ii., Part ii., of Dr Rashdall's " Universities of Europe." There are two short histories of the University by Maxwell Lyte (London, 1886) and Brodrick (London, 1886.).)

Documents relating to the University and Colleges of Cambridge. (London, 1852.)

Mullinger : The University of Cambridge from the Earliest Times to the Royal Injunctions of 1535. (Cambridge, 1873.)
In two subsequent volumes Mr Mullinger has continued the narrative to the latter half of the seventeenth century, and he has also written a short " History of the University of Cambridge." (Epochs of Church History. London, 1888.)

Gherardi : Statuti della università e studio Fiorentino. (Florence, 1881.)

Villanueva : Statutes of the University of Lerida in "Viage Literario á las Iglesias de España." T. xvi. (Madrid, 1851.)

Marcel Fournier : Les Statuts et Privilèges des Universités françaises depuis leur fondation jusqu'en 1789. (Paris, 1890-92.)

Dittrich und Spirk : Monumenta Historica Universitatis Pragensis. (Prague, 1830.)

Kink : Geschichte der Kaiserl. Univ. zu Wien. (Vienna, 1854.)

Hautz : Geschichte der Universität Heidelberg. (Mannheim, 1862.)

Vernulæus : Academia Lovaniensis. (Louvain, 1667.)

Molanus : Historiæ Lovaniensium, ed. De Ram. (Brussels, 1861.)

Zarncke : Die Statutenbücher der Univ. Leipzig. (Leipzig, 1861.)

——— Acta Rectorum Univ. Lipsiensis. (Leipzig, 1858.)

Evidence taken and received by the Scottish Universities Commissioners of 1826. (London, 1837.)

Innes : Fasti Aberdonenses. Spalding Club. (Aberdeen, 1854.)

INDEX

TURNBULL AND SPEARS, PRINTERS, EDINBURGH

98-170